THEORY, DOCTRINE AND PRACTICE

OF CONFLICT DE-ESCALATION

IN PEACEKEEPING OPERATIONS

The Canadian Peacekeeping Press
of
The Lester B. Pearson
Canadian International Peacekeeping Training Centre
Cornwallis Park, PO Box 100, Clementsport, NS B0S 1E0

Modern international stability operations frequently involve several warring factions, an unstable or non-existent truce, and a national theatre of operations. To deal with these operations there is a *New Peacekeeping Partnership:* The *New Peacekeeping Partnership* is the term applied to those organizations and individuals that work together to improve the effectiveness of modern peacekeeping operations. It includes the military; civil police; government and non-government agencies dealing with human rights and humanitarian assistance; diplomats; the media; and organizations sponsoring development and democratization programmes. The Pearson Peacekeeping Centre serves the *New Peacekeeping Partnership* by providing national and international participants with the opportunity to examine specific peacekeeping issues, and to update their knowledge of the latest peacekeeping practices.

Canadian Cataloguing in Publication Data

Last, David M.

Theory, doctrine and practice of conflict
de-escalation in peacekeeping operations

Includes bibliographical references.

ISBN 1-896551-08-4

1. International police. 2. War -- Termination. 3. Conflict management.
4. United Nations -- Armed Forces -- Case studies. I. Lester B. Pearson
Canadian International Peacekeeping Training Centre. II. Title.

JX1981.P7L37   1997   355.3'57   C96-930062-X

A thesis presented to the Faculty of the US Army Command and General Staff College in partial fulfilment of the requirements of the degree.

Printed by Brown Book Company Ltd., Toronto, ON

By David M. Last

Theory, Doctrine and Practice of Conflict De-Escalation in Peacekeeping Operations

The Canadian Peacekeeping Press

1997

The Lester B. Pearson
Canadian International Peacekeeping
Training Centre
President, Alex Morrison, MSC, CD, MA

The Pearson Peacekeeping Centre supports and enhances the Canadian contribution to international peace, security, and stability. The Centre conducts research and provides advanced training and educational programmes, and is a division of the Canadian Institute of Strategic Studies. The Canadian Peacekeeping Press is the publishing division of the Pearson Peacekeeping Centre.

The Centre (a division of the Canadian Institute of Strategic Studies), established by the Government of Canada in 1994, is funded, in part, by the Department of Foreign Affairs and International Trade and the Department of National Defence of Canada.

Le centre (une division de l'Institut canadien d'études stratégiques) à été établi par le Gouvernement du Canada en 1994. Le soutien financier de Centre provient, en partie, des ministères des Affaires étrangères et du commerce international et de la Défense nationale.

Canadian Peacekeeping Press publications include:

Facing the Future:
Proceedings of the 1996 Canada-Japan Conference
on Modern Peacekeeping (1997)

Seeds of Freedom:
Personal Reflections on the Dawning of Democracy (1996)

Analytic Approaches to the Study of Future Conflict (1996)

Pearson Paper #1: Peacekeeping and the Coming Anarchy (1996)

The Centre-Periphery Debate in International Security (1996)

Rapid Reaction Capabilities: Requirements and Prospects
*Les capacités de réaction rapide de l'ONU:
exigences et perspectives* (1996)

The New Peacekeeping Partnership (1995)

The Persian Excursion: The Canadian Navy in the Gulf War (1995)

Peacekeeping and International Relations (bi-monthly)

The Canadian and International Peacekeeping Review (forthcoming)

The Peacekeeping Profile (quarterly)

For publications information, please contact:

James Kiras, Publications Manager
The Pearson Peacekeeping Centre
Cornwallis Park, PO Box 100
Clementsport, NS B0S 1E0 CANADA
Tel: (902) 638-8611 ext. 161 Fax: (902) 638-8576
Email: jkiras@ppc.cdnpeacekeeping.ns.ca
Or visit the Pearson Peacekeeping Centre website:
http://www.cdnpeacekeeping.ns.ca

Acknowledgements

This study was supported by the Canadian Department of National Defence. Survey data was collected by ADGA Incorporated under a contract with the Directorate of Research and Development (Land), Department of National Defence, in 1994 (Reference Number W8477-93-CBAW), and by a research visit in which I participated.

This research was originally presented as a thesis at the United States Army Command and General Staff College in 1995.

I am grateful for the assistance of the many officers, soldiers, and civilians who have contributed interview material over the last five years. Many are listed as sources, while some have declined to be named. All the staff of the Combined Arms Research Library and Cheryl McLennan of the Canadian Defence Technical Information Service have been tremendously helpful. Dr. John Fishel, Mr. John Hunt and Lieutenant-Colonel Murray Swan offered valuable advice throughout. Susan McNish of the Canadian Institute of Strategic Studies and James Kiras of The Canadian Peacekeeping Press have been patient and persistent. Errors and omissions are mine alone.

Dorothyanne, Christina, Peter, and John have suffered stoically the long absences—mental and physical—occasioned by my work. For their patience and support I am always grateful.

Contents

Acknowledgements v

List of Figures vii

List of Tables viii

Chapter One: Peacekeeping and De-escalation 1

Chapter Two: Conflict Theory and De-escalation 14

Chapter Three: Peacekeeping Doctrine and De-escalation 43

Chapter Four: Combat and Contact Skills in Practice 67

Chapter Five: Orchestrating De-escalation Campaigns 90

Chapter Six: Winning the Peace 119

List of Abbreviations 132

Bibliography 134

List of Figures

1   Stages of De-escalation 3

2   Framework for Analysis of Third-Party Mediation 4

3   Developing Tactics, Techniques and Procedures 8

4   Dynamic Protraction Model of Conflict 22

5   Spectrum of Conflict De-escalation 25

6   American View of Peace Operations Environment 50

7   Comparative Approaches to Use of Force 52

8   British Concept of Consent and Use of Force 53

9   Nordic Sequence of Escalation 59

10 Combat and Contact Skills at the Tactical Level 61

11 Experience of Violence (Croatia) 77

12 Experience of Violence (Bosnia) 77

13 Use of Force by Peacekeepers 79

14 Comparison of Contact Experience by Rank 80

15 Communicating the Third Party's Intentions 99

16 Context of Negotiations 112

17 Contact Skills and Stages of De-escalation 122

List of Tables

1   Types of Violent Incident 6

2   Question Categories in the Eyre Survey 10

3   Causes of Escalation 21

4   Tactics Derived From Theory 37

5   Sources of Doctrine 44

6   Self-Defense and Use of Force 47

7   Individual Responses to Violent Situations 63

8   Types of Violence 68

9   Characteristics of Violent Incidents 75

Chapter One

Peacekeeping and De-Escalation

The gun that does not have to shoot is more eloquent than the gun that has to shoot, and above all, more eloquent than the gun which has shot.[1]

Salvador de Madariaga

This study is about the problem of de-escalation in peacekeeping operations. In war, soldiers are sent to defeat an enemy. In peace operations, soldiers are sent to help defeat a conflict. The peacekeeping equivalent of dead enemy soldiers and ground gained is violence abated and growing trust between former enemies. The task is not simple, and it has not received as much military attention as have the tasks of war.

Outline

This chapter presents a framework for analysis of the problem of de-escalation, based on theory, doctrine and practice. Chapter Two reviews selected conflict resolution theory to derive ideas about how peacekeepers can contribute to de-escalation. Chapter Three draws on existing and emerging military doctrine for peacekeeping and derives a range of tactics, techniques, and procedures which might be used to handle violent incidents. The fourth chapter uses surveys of operational experience to link the theory and doctrine. It suggests that the control of violent incidents at the tactical level (using predominantly combat techniques) should be more closely linked to systematic campaigns for the reduction of violence at the operational level, (using mainly contact techniques). The final chapter asks how contact and combat skills are orchestrated to achieve de-escalation at battalion and sector level. Campaigns to stop shooting, reduce seizures, prevent armed incursions, and achieve disengagement are assessed using factors which theory and doctrine suggest are important.

Background and Scope

Peacekeeping is the "prevention, containment, moderation and termination of hostilities between or within states through the medium of third party intervention."[2]

The moderation or de-escalation of hostilities occurs in the course of single incidents, as well as over time. For example, a shooting incident is defused by skillful intervention; over time the frequency and severity of such incidents also declines if a peacekeeping mission is successful. Situation reports, war diaries, and mission summaries show the de-escalation of hostilities over time, but do not give a clear picture of the actions which are taken by units and staff officers to de-escalate violent situations at the tactical level. The limitations of these documents confine the study to recent events where interviews help to identify de-escalation techniques at the tactical and operational level.

The study concerns current missions with armed troops, and focuses from unit (tactical) to sector and force headquarters (operational) levels. These are the United Nations Force in Cyprus (UNFICYP), United Nations Force in Lebanon (UNIFIL), United Nations Disengagement Observer Force (UNDOF), United Nations Protection Force (UNPROFOR), United Nations Operation in Mozambique (ONUMOZ), the second United Nations Operation in Somalia (UNOSOM II), and the United Nations Mission in Rwanda (UNAMIR).[3] This permits assessment of the combination of force deployment and negotiation to handle incidents. Most of the case studies and information come from UNFICYP and UNPROFOR, but the observations should be applicable to any mission with forces deployed. Only situations involving actual or threatened violence are considered, and the international (strategic) level is addressed only as a constraint on actions at lower levels. Insufficient data are available to determine the effect of actions on the number or severity of incidents over time, except in the short term. Logistics, administration, and support issues are not considered.

Three further limitations on the study stem from the nature of the data available and the dilemmas of an armchair peacekeeper. Details of the conduct of negotiations will not be addressed, although relevant references will be found in the footnotes. How peacekeepers negotiate is a book yet to be written. Second, particular techniques for handling incidents are not advocated. It is easy to be wise after the fact, and foolhardy to suggest techniques which might have worked under unique local circumstances which cannot be captured fully in a vignette. Third, the theoretical model of de-escalation extends beyond control of violence to restoration of a secure and stable peace, reconstruction of inter-communal ties and former enemies living happily ever after. There is a dearth of anecdotal data on the latter stages of the de-escalation process. Few conflicts have story-book endings. The investigation is therefore confined to military efforts to control and de-escalate violence.

This study is intended for students and practitioners of peacekeeping and conflict resolution. It is assumed that they will have some background knowledge or personal experience of peacekeeping missions, and the history of individual missions will not be treated in detail. Others have covered that ground. On the other hand, few military or civilian participants in peacekeeping operations seem to have a background in the theory and practice of conflict resolution. This study can fill an important void by linking conflict resolution theory and research to military doctrine and practice for peacekeeping in protracted social conflicts.

Theoretical Framework

The theoretical framework for this study links the academic concept of peacekeeping as a form of third party intervention to assist conflict resolution to the military doctrine of levels of war. This linkage is based on one key assumption, and generates several others.

The key assumption for this framework is that UN forces are deployed as part of a coherent strategy to control and prevent violent conflict through coordinated third party intervention.[4] Assuming coherence, the strategy is pursued at the strategic, operational and tactical levels across a spectrum of de-escalation with the ultimate aim of restoring a peace acceptable to all parties.[5]

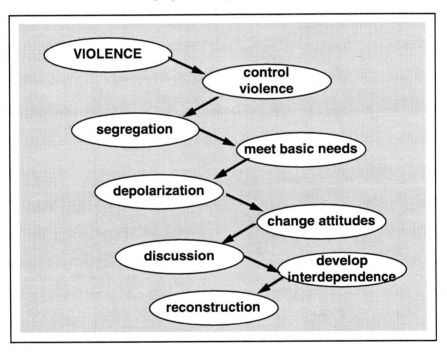

Figure 1: Stages of De-escalation
Source: Ron Fisher, 1986

At the **strategic** level, the UN, states, and non-state actors attempt to contain, moderate, and terminate hostilities by diplomatic, economic, and military means. This activity sets the environment within which violence is handled at the operational and tactical levels. De-escalation might encompass several stages, such as those described by Fisher (Figure 1).[6]

At the **operational** level, a force headquarters translates a strategy of third party intervention into the deployment of forces to control and prevent violence. The campaign plan at the operational level sets the conditions for success in the prevention, containment and moderation of violence at the tactical level. The "enemy" is violent conflict and the force commander's "allies" in defeating it are the opposing forces. The mediation paradigm described by Wall[7] is illustrated in Figure 2; it describes the environment in which peacekeepers operate. According to Prein's contingency model of conflict intervention,[8] the effectiveness of an intervention is influenced by the context of the conflict, the characteristics of the parties to the conflict, the nature of the conflict, and the intervention strategy. These are the key factors for assessing tactics, techniques, and procedures used in conflict de-escalation. They will be referred to again in the final chapter.

At the **tactical** level, units and staffs interact with the belligerents and civil populations both to prevent further violence and to rebuild normal life, which may include a return to peaceful inter-communal relations. To accomplish these tasks, formed units have weapons for self-defence and self-protection, logistic support, and interpersonal skills. Beyond this they may draw on the resources of support or service support units, military or civilian observers or civilian agencies.

The central problem at the tactical level is balancing the deployment of forces against direct contact and negotiations with the combatants.[9] Models of negotiated conflict resolution from social psychology and industrial relations normally omit the possibility of armed coercion, with which peacekeepers must deal at the tactical level.[10] International relations models, on the other hand, include the potential for coercion, but focus on conflict structures at the strategic level and offer little guidance to the officer negotiating at platoon, company or battalion level.[11]

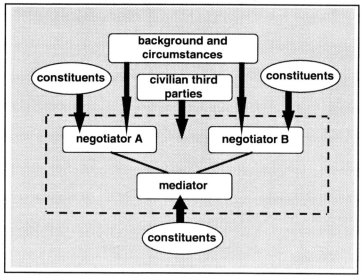

Figure 2: Framework for Analysis of Third-Party Mediation

Further assumptions are necessary in order to make use of this framework. It is assumed that the insights of social science theory derived from experiments and real-world observations are applicable. To the extent that people in conflict behave in similar ways across cultural boundaries, this assumption is valid. To the extent that patterns of conflict are culturally unique, it must be amended.

It is assumed that insights from international relations theory are relevant. Violence and coercion are present in both international and internal conflicts in which peacekeepers frequently find themselves.

It is assumed that de-escalation is achieved by two sorts of action in peacekeeping operations: "defensive" actions which are aimed at stopping direct violence (shooting and moving by either side against the other); and "offensive" actions which are directed against the causes of the conflict and include the building of trust and confidence. Because of the focus on controlling and de-escalating violent incidents, the emphasis will clearly be on defensive activities; offensive action generally requires security and stability for some time.

Definitions

The key terms used in this study are: peacekeeping; tactics, techniques, and procedures; violent incidents; campaigns; and de-escalation.

The most widely used definition of peacekeeping is the one found in Liu's unofficial UN history of peacekeeping, The Blue Helmets:

> As the United Nations practice has evolved over the years, a peace-keeping operation has come to be defined as an operation involving military personnel, but without enforcement powers, undertaken by the United Nations to help maintain or restore international peace and security in areas of conflict.[12]

Rather than this, I have chosen the older definition of the International Peace Academy cited earlier in this chapter. It encompasses both the holding missions common prior to 1988, and more ambitious attempts to de-escalate tensions and restore peace. These rely on effective military and civilian cooperation, and cannot be thought of primarily as operations involving military personnel, although armed forces are an essential component.

Tactics is "the art and science of employing available means to win battles and engagements."[13] Further, it is the "ordered arrangement and manoeuvre of units in relation to each other, to the enemy, or both, to utilize their full potential."[14] A battle is "a series of related engagements, involving larger forces, possibly affecting the course of the campaign."[15] In peacekeeping terms, an engagement is a single meeting, intervention, or deployment, localized in time and place and executed by a single level of command. Engagements are normally short; in peacekeeping missions they occur mainly at battalion or sector level and below. The peacekeeping equivalent of a battle is a series of related meetings, interventions or deployments which may involve several levels of command or several different types of assets but which have a common purpose and together may affect the local or wider course of the conflict.

Techniques are "the detailed methods for accomplishing tasks. They are not the only way to do a task or the way a task must be done. They can be changed as needed." A procedure is "a standard and detailed course of action that describes how to perform a certain task" (for example, a call for artillery fire or response to a telephoned bomb threat).[16] In this study, the terms "skills" and "techniques" are used interchangeably in a more general sense than common in military doctrine. Procedures are addressed by standing orders and terms of reference which are specific to missions and theatres, such as the format for reporting mines, shelling and sniping.[17]

Table 1: Types of Violent Incident

air attack
air threat or demonstration
indirect fire
direct fire
ambush
sniper fire
active mining
drive-by shooting
physical attack on installation
projectiles thrown
moves forward in force
unauthorized construction
restriction of movement
personal threat, intimidation
kidnapping or hostage-taking
riots or civilian violence
passive aid to violence

Tactics, techniques, and procedures used by peacekeepers to deal with these violent situations include, *inter alia*, applying rules of engagement (ROE), conducting "cordon and search" operations to seize weapons, responding to direct or indirect fire, securing areas, and protecting the peacekeeping force.[18] These are combat skills. Investigation, negotiation, mediation, arbitration, conciliation, and other "contact skills" are also tactics for the de-escalation of violent situations.[19]

The interaction of these two types of tactics, rather than the use of individual tactics to resolve incidents, will be the focus, for reasons mentioned above.

Violent incidents faced in peacekeeping missions are just one form of engagement. For the purposes of this study "engagements" will be chosen which involve the types of violent situations commonly identified in the after-action reports of complex peacekeeping missions. These are listed in Table 1.[20]

Campaigns are planned and executed at the operational level— normally the sector or force headquarters. Campaigns related to de-escalation which are routinely pursued include: disengaging forces; establishing buffer zones; preventing armed incursions; stopping persistent violations of a cease-fire by direct or indirect fire; reducing hostage-taking and seizures; and demilitarizing areas.

De-escalation is the successive reduction of tension, hostility and potential or actual violence. It occurs in the life of a single engagement, and can be traced in the pattern of events over time.

Research Questions

The central research question is: How can peacekeepers control and de-escalate violent situations? This is related to the tactical problem of combining negotiations and force deployment to achieve the mission, de-escalate violence, and minimize risk to the force. The research problem is to identify how units and staffs control and de-escalate violent situations while supporting the larger purpose for which they are there. Strategic, operational, and tactical levels are relevant, although the focus will be on the latter two.

This gives rise to four questions about the process of conflict control. First, what do peacekeepers in units actually do (at the tactical level)? Second (still at the tactical level) how do battalions and companies handle violent incidents? Third, how are different sorts of violence dealt with at the operational level? And finally, how do force and sector headquarters plan for de-escalation and the control of violent incidents?

Research Design and Data Collection

Military tactics are derived from doctrine. Doctrine builds on principles derived from theory, which is generalized from experience. This relationship is shown in Figure 3. The research follows this structure, beginning with theoretical and doctrinal insights, collecting data on current experiences, and interpreting those experiences in the light of theory and doctrine. One of the weaknesses of current doctrine is that it does not draw on theory and generalizations about conflict resolution which have been derived from our peacekeeping experience and related civilian endeavours.[21]

The contingency approach to third party intervention is well established[22] and has explanatory power in experimental situations[23] and in international relations involving coercion.[24] It suggests that the outcome of third party intervention is contingent upon the context of the conflict, the nature of the parties to the dispute, the nature of the conflict itself, and the intervention strategy of the third party.[25] This provides the framework for data collection.

Deriving tactics, techniques, and procedures therefore requires four steps. First, how can we assess what we are doing now? This demands theoretical and doctrinal filters through which to examine our experience. Second, what is our current experience of violent incidents? This demands data collection from relevant missions. The less complete the data set, the less comprehensive will be the recommendations about specific tactics. Third, which tactics work and why? The theoretical and doctrinal filters established in the first step should allow us to determine or at least speculate on the reasons for success or failure, but it will not be possible to recommend tactics for specific situations for reasons mentioned above. This will get us to the fourth step, describing effective tactics in general terms, including the balance of negotiation and force deployment.

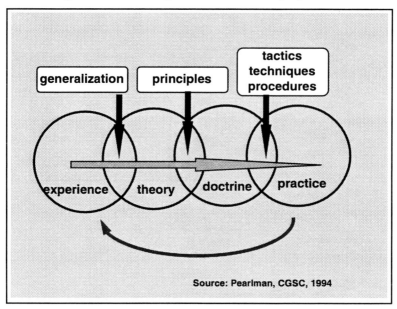

Source: Pearlman, CGSC, 1994

Figure 3: Developing Tactics, Techniques and Procedures

What violent situations do peacekeepers face? This question can be answered by examining after-action reports of units and situation reports from a variety of missions. It would be useful at some point to quantify the level and type of violence by mission over time, but that will not be necessary for this study. Here it will suffice to identify types of violent incidents and campaigns to address them. This has already been done by a survey of after-action reports and lessons-learned documents from Canadian and American sources.

What do peacekeepers do at various rank levels? This question can be answered directly with survey research which has already been completed. These can be used to identify common actions and experiences with rank levels, to differentiate between the types of activities undertaken by soldiers, sub-unit and unit leaders.

Results of three Canadian surveys of peacekeepers are available: Dr. Frank Pinch's Human Resources Study; Land Force Command's (LFC) Reserve Survey; and Dr. Ken Eyre's survey for the Directorate of Research and Development (Land). In addition, about 40 hours of videotaped interviews with key commanders and staff of 12[ieme] Regiment Blindé du Canada (12 RBC) are available to provide personal perspectives and notes on specific types of operations at the unit level.

Dr. Pinch conducted interviews with about 200 returning peacekeepers from Yugoslavia in 1993-94. These were personal interviews with open-ended questions focusing on unit preparation and personnel support. The general headings of the Pinch survey include: demographic data (9 questions); selection of units and personnel (12 questions); preparation for peacekeeping (8 questions); personnel support structures (4 multiple questions); force management and conventional readiness (8 questions); military service and career (five questions); and cohesion, morale and satisfaction (9 multiple questions).

The LFC survey was administered to about 250 reservists of Land Force Quebec Area (SQFT) and Land Force Western Area (LFWA) in 1993-94 with the aim of ensuring equitable employment for reservists and operational effectiveness of units. It consists of demographic data, a section on rank qualification and motivation to be completed prior to deployment, and a section on rank and employment to be completed on return.

Neither of these surveys will answer the questions, although the Pinch survey may yield useful insights because of open-ended questions.

The Eyre survey was administered to about 1,200 soldiers from three units and supporting organizations of Canada's 5[ieme] Brigade (5 GBMC) in 1994.[26] Ninety-six questions are arranged in nine groups (below) with an additional four open-ended questions on best/worst and most memorable incidents. The 96 questions have yes/no answers. The results of open ended questions are summarized in separate documents.[27] The resulting data base has been queried concerning activities undertaken at each rank level. While the data base is not as complete as could be hoped for, it offers the best empirical measure of activities by rank. The basic combat skills reflected in groups 2 and 3 (conflict and use of force) are higher for other ranks than for officers, while the incidence of involvement in negotiations (group 6) varies directly with rank.

How do battalions and companies handle violent incidents? When faced with the sorts of incidents listed above, how do companies and battalions combine combat and contact skills to respond, and what are the effects of their actions? The aim was to collect as many "cases" as possible from as wide a variety of

Table 2: Question Categories in the Eyre survey

1. basic skills
2. conflict
3. use of force
4. casualties
5. media
6. negotiations
7. operations
8. work with other organizations
9. miscellaneous

circumstances as possible. In practice, the majority of useful ones has come from UNPROFOR and UNFICYP. While this lends a certain cohesion to the study, it does beg questions about the transferability of results, as mentioned above. Each "case" consists of a description of the incident, the background to the incident, the nature of the parties involved, the UN response to the incident, and the outcome of the incident. These variables have been chosen according to the theoretical framework outlined above.

A collection of illustrative scenarios or incidents drawn from the recent experiences of peacekeepers helps to identify tactics and techniques in use. Placing each incident in a contingency framework helps to explain why an incident was successfully handled using certain techniques, and may help identify the consequences of using or not using other techniques. This is done mainly in Chapters Four and Five.

The most important source of information about tactics for de-escalation is the recent experience of peacekeepers in complex missions. Their successes and failures in dealing with violent incidents should guide training and doctrine. The collection plan was intended to overcome some specific problems, and relied mainly on interviews with officers who have recently served in UN missions. About 180 vignettes were collected. Those which have been used can be substantiated by other interview or documentary sources, and yield useful insights within the scope of the model. I must emphasize that there are many other useful insights from vignettes which have not been cited in this study.

How are de-escalation campaigns conducted at battalion level and higher? This question can be broken down into two parts. First, how are combat and contact skills orchestrated to achieve de-escalation? Second, what opportunities are there for military forces to take "offensive" action against conflict? This will be answered inductively using cases selected from the collection of vignettes and followed up with interviews and document searches. This inductive process is not ideal. It leaves a lot of gaps and leads to observations which may appear naïve to more experienced peacekeepers. It is hoped that this will also yield some insights in the tradition of inductive hypotheses.

These four steps result in conclusions about the role of combat and contact tactics, techniques, and procedures for handling incidents and campaigns, related to the nature of the conflict, the context of the conflict, and the nature of the parties to the conflict. Concrete illustrations have been drawn mainly from UNPROFOR.

The method outlined above is not a certain recipe for deriving useful tactics, techniques, and procedures for peacekeepers. What is missing is quantities of realistic data on individual incidents from current peacekeeping missions. Part of that gap will be filled by surveys now being sent out by the UN's Department of Peacekeeping Operations. The remainder will have to await serious field research.

Conclusion

The insights of theory and doctrine are a useful starting point for collecting and assessing data from contemporary missions. This study will not provide hard answers about the best way to get past a checkpoint or avoid becoming a hostage. But it should provide insights to commanders, staff, practitioners, and academics who are battling the common problem of de-escalating violence in today's complex peacekeeping missions.

Endnotes

1   Salvador de Madariaga, Director of the Disarmament Section of the League of Nations Secretariat, 1925.

2   International Peace Academy, Peacekeeper's Handbook (New York: Pergamon, 1984), 7.

3   United Nations, United Nations Peacekeeping: Information Notes—Update May 1994 (UN NY: Peace and Security Programmes Section, 1994).

4   Jaque Grinberg, Civil Affairs HQ UNPROFOR, "The UNPROFOR Mandate," (unpublished paper) 14 February 1994, 1. This assumption may not always be supported by actual mandates:

> "...a plethora of Security Council Resolutions have arguably complicated, rather than enlightened, the work of UNPROFOR and other engaged international institutions. It can be argued that at this moment, in effect UNPROFOR has no mandate. What it has is a menu of not entirely consistent objectives and no unifying plan to prioritize and direct the work..."

5   "United Nations Department of Peacekeeping Operations, Command and Control Review, 9 November 1993, presents the grand strategic level (security council) strategic level (Secretary-General, UN Secretariat), operational level (Force commander with military, political and civilian components) and the tactical level (units, UN agencies and NGOs).

6   Ronald J. Fisher, "The Potential for Peacebuilding: Forging a Bridge from Peacekeeping to Peacemaking," Peace and Change, 1993.

7   James A. Wall, "Mediation: An Analysis, Review and Proposed Research," Journal of Conflict Resolution, 25:1 (March 1981), 157-181. The diagram in Figure 2 is actually adapted from Hugo Prein, "A Contingency Approach to Conflict Intervention," Group and Organization Studies, 9:1 (March 1984), 81-102.

8   Hugo Prein, "A Contingency Approach to Conflict Intervention," Group and Organization Studies 9:1 (March 1984), 81-102.

9   This is well expressed in Chapter Four of A. B. Fetherston, Toward a Theory of United Nations Peacekeeping (University of Bradford: Peace Research Report Number 31, February 1993).

10   For example, Ottomar J. Bartos (1968) "How Predictable are Negotiations?" Journal of Conflict Resolution, 11:4, 481-496; Jeffrey W. Eiseman (1978) "Reconciling 'Incompatible' Positions," The Journal of Applied Behavioural Science, Vol 14, number 2, 133-150; Roger Fisher (1986) "Dealing with Conflict Among Individuals: Are There Common Principles?" Psycho-analytic Inquiry, 6:2, 143-153 and Roger Fisher, William Ury, and Bruce Patton, (1991) Getting to Yes: Negotiating Agreement Without Giving In, Second Edition (Harmondsworth: Penguin) amongst others.

11   For example, Jacob Bercovitch (1986) "International Mediation: A Study of the Incidence, Strategies and Conditions of Successful Outcomes," Cooperation and Conflict, 21:3 (September), 155-168; or Glenn H. Snyder, and Paul Diesing, Conflict Among Nations: Bargaining, Decision Making and System Structure in International Crises (Princeton, NJ: Princeton University Press, 1977).

12   The Blue Helmets: A Review of United Nations Peace-Keeping (New York: United Nations Department of Public Information, 1990), 4.

13   United States Army Field Manual 100-5, Operations (Headquarters, Department of the Army, June 1993), 6-3.

14   US Army FM 7-20, 2-6.

15   Ibid.

16   The American Center for Army Lessons Learned (CALL) does not distinguish between tactics, techniques, and procedures, but refers to them collectively as TTP. These definitions are from FM 7-20 page 2-6.

17   Examples of troop handbooks issued in-theatre include Memento sur l'espace yougoslave, République Français, Ministère de la défence (Février 1994); Troop Information Pamphlet for the Balkan Peninsula, 1992 (Unpublished paper issued to US troops); V Corps Operation Provide Promise Deployment Handbook. Typical procedural checklists include meeting the media, reporting overflights, shelling and sniping reports, injury and accident reports, and so on.

18   Center for Army Lessons Learned (CALL) Newsletter 93-8: Operations Other Than War, Volume IV: Peace Operations (US Army Combined Arms Command, Fort Leavenworth, Kansas, December 1993).

19   Peacekeeper's Handbook, 273-274.

20   Drawn from Canadian and American after-action reports.

21   A.B. Fetherston, Toward a Theory of UN Peacekeeping, (Department of Peace Studies, University of Bradford, Peace Research Report No. 31, February 1993); and D. M. Last, "Peacekeeping Doctrine and Conflict Resolution Techniques," Paper presented to the Biennial Conference of the Inter-University Seminar on Armed Forces and Society, Baltimore, MD, 23 October 1993 (Forthcoming in Armed Forces and Society).

22   Hugo Prein, "A Contingency Approach to Conflict Intervention," Group and Organization Studies 9:1 (March 1984), 81-102.

23   Ronald J. Fisher and Loraleigh Keashly, "The Potential Complementarity of Mediation and Consultation within a Contingency Model of Third Party Intervention," Journal of Peace Research, 28:1 (February, 1991), 29-42.

24   Bercovitch. 1986, op. cit.

25 James A. Wall, Jr., "Mediation: An Analysis, Review, and Proposed Research," Journal of Conflict Resolution 25:1 (March 1981), 157-180.

26 This research was conducted by Dr. K. C. Eyre of ADGA Inc., under sponsorship of the Directorate of Research and Development (Land). Results are made available through ADGA.

27 K. C. Eyre, ADGA Systems International, "Anecdotal Data from CANBAT 2 (12ᵉ RBC) General Peacekeeping Survey," and "Anecdotal Data from UNPROFOR OP HARMONY CANBAT 1 (1 R22ᵉR) General Peacekeeping Survey," Peacekeeping Interview Program (Ottawa, October 1993-April 1994).

Chapter Two

Conflict Theory and De-Escalation[1]

Conflict is an illness, and like any other illness it requires the correct treatment to cure it. Conflict treatment therefore requires as much careful study and research as does conflict itself.[2]

A great deal of careful study and research has been devoted to conflict treatment. Too little of it is read by soldiers. This chapter draws from theory and empirical research to suggest some of the things which might be done by peacekeepers to de-escalate conflict.

Because of the types of violence peacekeepers face, theory and research on intergroup violence is the most germane. Findings suggest that concrete steps like physical separation must be taken, but also that more difficult solutions like attitude change must occur over the long term. Research also suggests limitations on the military contribution to conflict de-escalation. Finally, both theory and practice suggest that timing and "target selection" are crucial for effective de-escalation.

Conflict resolution theory builds on research on collective experience and understanding of processes for controlling and managing conflict. A model of peacekeeping as third party intervention and a spectrum of conflict de-escalation at the strategic, operational, and tactical levels is derived. In the next chapter, this will be linked to doctrine based on peacekeeping experience to derive a list of functions which contribute to de-escalation.

What Sort of Conflict Theory?

What sort of theory about conflict is appropriate as a starting point to understand the de-escalation of violent incidents faced by peacekeepers? It should meet three criteria. First, it should be relevant to conflict between groups at the level at which peacekeeping forces must work. This means it must address the operational and tactical level of violence—violence between groups and individuals rather than the causes of wars between states. Second, it must be relevant to the causes of violent behaviour of individuals acting on their own behalf and of those acting within a structure like a militia or military force. Third, it must be relevant to violence directed towards another combatant and towards an intervening force.

Theory About Conflict Between States

Some of the conflicts in which peacekeepers intervene occur between states. A large body of theory exists about the nature of interstate conflict. This describes the conflict of rational or constrained actors across national boundaries.

Morgenthau, for example, addresses classic issues of power politics in an international setting: the sources and elements of national power; restraints on national power; and problems of disarmament, security, and diplomacy in the pursuit of peace.[3] Although not oblivious to the inner workings of states, the modern fathers of international relations as a discipline reified the state the better to study it.[4] By treating conflict as the product of rational decisions by unitary actors, they excluded many of the causes of violence that face peacekeepers today.

Now war as a rational instrument may be a thing of the past; Michael Howard writes that: "It is quite possible that war in the sense of major, organized armed conflict between highly developed societies may not recur . . . ."[5] Yet organized violence between groups will almost certainly continue. The weapons in these struggles can range from small arms to heavy artillery. The tactics range from those of bandit gangs to those of higly organized formations. Violence between communities within many states has demonstrably increased since the collapse of the bipolar world. These types of conflicts are not new.

If we do not understand these conflicts, armies which have evolved as rational instruments of state power are at a disadvantage in dealing with them. The characteristics of protracted social conflicts will determine the ways in which armed forces can be used to assist in their control and prevention. Theory and research pertinent to violent conflict between groups and individuals should guide military understanding of de-escalation.

The Nature of Protracted Social Conflict

Protracted social conflicts rest on underlying social, political, and economic disparities. Underdevelopment and the unequal distribution of resources is often exacerbated by multiethnic and communal cleavages.[6] In Cyprus for example, the fact that Greek Cypriots tend to control businesses and Turkish Cypriots tend to work the land led some Turkish-Cypriot farmers to feel exploited by Greek-Cypriot businessmen. This is related to deep-rooted insecurities based on human needs.

Competition for resources to meet basic needs is a growing source of conflict between identity groups. In the Middle East, water is a critical resource in short supply. Arab and Israeli communities both need more each year, but water tables are declining.[7]

A group's need for recognition and identity in a separate community is another source of conflict. The most useful unit of analysis for these conflicts is frequently not the state, but the ethnic community or identity group.

Competition over scarce resources is heightened by natural disasters like drought, famine, flood, and soil erosion. Indeed conflicts with their roots in a deteriorating environment may be the wave of the future.[8] In "The Coming Anarchy" Robert Kaplan offers a sobering vision of refugee tides washing across fragile state boundaries;[9] environmental disasters cause migration, aggravating ethnic tensions.[10] Nazli Choucri and Robert North investigated the link between what they called the "master variables"—population, resources and technology. When population combines with technology to increase the demand on resources, "lateral pressure" causes conflicts within and between communities and states.[11]

These are not conflicts which can be confined in time: they last for generations, subsiding and re-emerging over centuries. In Burundi, the Hutu and Tutsi have long been adversaries; in Cyprus, periodic violence has erupted since the Ottoman colonization in 1570. Resolution cannot be quick and may never be permanent.

The Relevance of Protracted Social Conflict to Peacekeeping

When conflicts occur between states with sovereign control over their populations and armies, the problem of conflict de-escalation and resolution rests largely at the strategic level. A functioning state can be treated as a unitary actor. When a state or its citizens violate international law then political, military, and economic instruments of influence can be used at the strategic level to bring about change.

Third parties intervening in protracted social conflicts have three distinctly different challenges. The first is that protracted social conflicts undermine state power. The nominal authority of the state is fragmented by the competing claims of ethnic or political groups within the state or transcending state borders.[12] For third parties intervening to control and prevent violent conflict while a political settlement is reached, they must now seek to control the sources of escalation and violence at multiple levels, from individual and group violence to the national level. In effect, third parties have an almost infinite array of constituents to satisfy.

The second challenge for third parties intervening in protracted social conflicts is that the causes of conflict are more intractable and difficult to assess. States articulate war aims; groups and individuals respond to numerous pressures which are different for each and change over time.

The third challenge is that protracted social conflicts are often defined in zero-sum terms. Any gain by one party may be perceived by the other as a categorical loss to itself, even when the issues are not distributive in nature.

Prevalence of Protracted Social Conflicts

Protracted social conflicts are the dominant sort of violence with which the international community must now deal. It might be argued that this has been the case since the Second World War. Istvan Kende's summary of conflicts in the twentieth century shows the preponderance of internal conflicts, many with the characteristics Azar describes.[13] Bloomfield's CASCON data-base describes 63 post-Second World War conflicts of which 45 are categorized as internal or civil wars.[14] Brogan's guide to world conflict since 1945 points to the wide dispersion of conflict, its persistence over time, and the involvement of ethnic, cultural, and resource factors in perpetuating cycles of violence.[15]

Although protracted social conflict is widespread and outbreaks of violence frequent since the Second World War, the patterns of violent ethno-political conflict vary widely by region. One-sixth of the world's population (or about 915 million people) identifies with one of the 233 groups identified by Gurr's study of minorities at risk. The greatest concentration of minorities at risk was found in Africa south of the Sahara with 74 minority groups and 42 percent of the regional population at risk. The western democracies and Latin America had the smallest percentage—at about 11 percent each.[16] Africa, Southwest Asia, Eastern Europe, and the far east are all zones of risk for minority groups. Every form of ethno-political conflict has increased sharply since the 1950s: nonviolent political action by the 233 communal groups more than doubled between 1950 and 1990, and violent protest and rebellion both quadrupled.[17]

There is no question that protracted social conflict between identity groups is the dominant form of conflict in the modern world, whether these coincide with national boundaries or occur within states. This is not to say that conflicts between sovereign states are unimportant, but for the purposes of this study, the focus will be on ethnopolitical and social conflicts of the sort which characterize today's complex peacekeeping missions.

Causes of Violence

What are the causes of these conflicts, and what do these causes indicate about the ways in which conflicts can be controlled or de-escalated by third parties? Sandole has identified six groups of causal factors in violence based on an extensive survey of empirical and experimental research. His framework is useful; each group of causal factors suggests actions which a third party might take to attenuate violence and its causes.

Individual Mechanisms Related to Violence

There are identifiable causes of violent behaviour in individuals which must be addressed if individual acts of violence are to be countered. John Burton, a former diplomat and doyen of peace studies, identifies the individual as the single most important independent variable, because individuals appear at every level of aggregation as actors and decision-makers.[18]

John Paul Scott, a behavioural psychologist, argues that fighting is a physiological response learned through success: "We find that [an individual's] motivation for fighting is strongly increased by success, and that the longer success continues, the stronger the motivation becomes."[19] It is possible that a series of local successes will make militiamen and local commanders more intransigent and more likely to seek their objectives with force. Local violence is also related to the use of alcohol or drugs in many cases, and violent responses may be partly conditioned by them.

Anthropologists and social psychologists can offer useful insights about individual behaviour. Bandura suggests that the physical response of aggressiveness is conditioned by social learning.[20] Koestler links social learning to transcendence of the self through identification with a social organization, whether tribe, church, nation, flag, or ideal.[21] Social restraints on individual behaviour are lifted by surrendering responsibility for individual actions to the collective identity. Peter Loizos has described how this process takes hold in an individual caught up in the generalizing nature of ethnic violence. The key factors in one case drawn from the Cyprus conflict appear to be: the selective history taught by nationalists; the example of nation-state behaviour; local ideas of will, power, domination, and revenge; and the logic of ethnic conflict as collectivist and nonspecific—"us" against "them"— which absolves the perpetrator of responsibility for his actions and makes any of "them" a legitimate target in atonement for the actions of their countrymen.[22]

To the extent that individual tendencies toward violence are learned responses, they may be modified through learning.[23] However, this may be overly optimistic. The experience of protracted social conflicts is that modifying patterns of social learning can take generations.

Two other causes of violence at the individual level stand out from research. The first is dissonance, or discrepancies between preferred and actual states of affairs. Cognitive dissonance gives rise to anxiety, which can be managed by avoidance, reassessment, or changing the actual state of affairs. This last might be done violently.[24]

A close causal connection has been established between frustration and aggression, if aggression is defined comprehensively. This has been established in experimental settings since Dollard's pioneering work in the 1930s.[25] Social scientists such as Galtung have built on these ideas. Galtung suggests that "structural violence," or unequal access to the means of reducing differences between perceived and actual states of affairs,[26] may be a significant source of frustration, which could give rise to individual "anomic" violence or to collective violence in a social setting.

These causes of violence suggest several important steps for soldiers on the front line of conflict control.

First, if there is a physiological mechanism which heightens aggression in individuals according to a learned stimulus (like the presence of a traditional enemy) then physical separation of belligerents is an important part of de-escalation, especially when tensions are high. Bringing them together again must be done with due care and attention to the risk of a violent response to the opposing force.

Second, education about the learned targets of hostility may play a role in de-escalating violence. This may be initially incompatible with mistrust and physical separation, but should be part of the campaign plan.

Third, if individuals respond violently to frustrated needs, then meeting those needs may reduce violent behaviour. To the extent that an intervening force is perceived as helping satisfy basic needs, it is less likely to be a target of violence itself. However, if it is perceived to be contributing to differences between desired and actual state of affairs (such as equality with another group), then it may quickly become a target. When the actual posture and tasks of the intervening force cannot be changed, or when misperception of the force's role is to blame, information might be used to reduce the frustration and dissonance experienced by belligerents.

Denial of Basic Needs

A hierarchy of human needs was postulated by Maslow as a primary source of both individual and group motivation.[27] These comprise survival needs (food, shelter, safety, and reproduction), social needs (identity and purpose), and higher-order needs (self-actualization). In the most violent stages of a conflict, many of the combatants are engaged in pursuit of survival needs; as the violence dies down, they are likely to be more concerned with social needs. This may make combatants less willing to accept imposed solutions over time.

Frustration/Aggression

Galtung's analysis of structural violence suggests that actors with mixed status—high on some indicators but low on others—are most likely to respond violently. For example, a numerically superior group with a declining share of a society's wealth, or a wealthy group with little political power, or a militarily strong group with little economic and political power—these would be candidates for violent response.[28]

Davis's relative deprivation (J-curve) analysis suggests that violence is more likely when expectations have been raised and then not fulfilled than when expectations and performance are both low. He links frustration of substantive needs (Maslow's physical, social and self-actualizing needs) to the conversion of non-violent or constructive conflict into aggressive or violent conflict.[29]

These explanations have relevance for soldiers facing units and formations in peacekeeping missions. Factions which are powerful and well-armed but receive no official recognition suffer from "rank disequilibrium"; they may be more difficult to deal with, and more prone to violence. Factions which have been accustomed to having their own way may be particularly difficult after an unexpected set-back.

Intransigence is likely to turn to violence if food sources, security, or identity are directly threatened.

Ethnocentrism and Realpolitik

That every identity group needs enemies to encourage internal cohesion is an old hypothesis (Sandole refers to it as "the oldest hypothesis in politics")[30] which has been given new currency by the explosion of ethnic rivalries. Conflict between groups is, according to this view, partly a result of weaknesses within groups.[31] The urge to seek and exploit differences between "them" and "us," reserving aggression for "them" may be universal.[32]

There is always a risk that a third party intervening in conflict can quickly become identified by both sides as the enemy, without being sufficiently threatening to cause rapprochement between the belligerent communities. To the extent that an intervening force can make itself useful, meeting some of the basic needs of the belligerent forces and their constituent communities, this problem may be forestalled.

Gurr describes empirical correlates of communal groups' grievances and demands. The strongest cause of struggle for political and economic rights is evident political and economic discrimination based on cultural differences. Ecological and demographic stress exacerbates demands for economic and political rights. The strongest factor linked to demands for autonomy is historical autonomy.[33]

Gurr's findings are relevant to any warning system attempting to identify potential sources of future inter-ethnic tension or struggles for autonomy. They also suggest that establishing and protecting minority rights is an important step in forestalling violent demands. In many settings, it appears that individual human rights are not seen as a substitute for collective minority rights. Majorities may support universal individual rights, while minorities seek a distinct identity and special status. Finding mechanisms to permit group identity for minorities without threatening other groups is particularly challenging in intermingled populations, where the balance changes with even slight boundary changes.

Hostility Spiral, Over-perception and Over-reaction

Once engaged in a conflict, there is a tendency for the actions of the other party to be perceived as hostile, even when they are devoid of hostile intent. Hostile acts are magnified and the response is correspondingly hostile. This self-fulfilling cycle of over-perception and over-reaction tends to reward and reinforce hard-liners. Moderates, whose loyalty and judgement may already be under attack, are further undermined.[34] This problem introduces the causes and correlates of escalation and de-escalation, from which additional deductions about peacekeeping tasks can be drawn.

Escalation and De-escalation

Escalation occurs when a conflict increases in intensity, or when the incidents associated with the conflict occur more frequently. Tactics used in the conflict become more serious and potentially more injurious, the number of issues proliferates, and parties become increasingly absorbed in the conflict. Self-interest may be subordinated to inflicting harm on the other party, as goals shift, influenced by the conflict.[36] Table 3 lists causes of escalation identified by James Wall and Rhonda Callister.[37]

Table 3: Causes of Escalation

predestination (conflicts have a predisposition to escalate)
cultural differences
history of antagonism
parties unaware of costs
parties not concerned with costs
no limit to actions
insecure self-images
uncertain status differences
poor socialization
no experience with crises
weak social bonds
mild power advantage
perception of power advantage
motivation to win (or not to lose)
uncertainty
lack of identification with other
festering resentment
inability to escape conflict
long, injurious stalemate

Source: Wall and Callister (1994)

These causes suggest some actions which might be taken by third parties to limit the degree to which violent conflicts escalate. For example, making the costs of the conflict explicit by broadcasting information, attempting to preserve or restore bonds between communities (through family visits, exchanges, and so on), or offsetting real or perceived power advantages might address some of the causes of escalation. Most causes of escalation, however, are beyond the immediate influence of third party intervention, because escalation occurs in the context of a conflict which is not yet ripe for third party intervention.

Few of the causes of de-escalation are the reciprocal of escalation causes. Anticipation of a common enemy can cause rapprochement. Stalemate and fatigue, the cure of time, is often a precursor to de-escalation, as is impending or recent disaster. Voluntary yielding, a change of goals, or conciliatory gestures can accelerate de-escalation.[37] None of these is within the power of third parties to command, but each represents an indicator of auspicious circumstances to attempt de-escalation, and a goal for modifying belligerents' behaviour. Several of them are evident in the campaigns discussed in Chapter Five.

Models of De-escalation

The problem of escalation and de-escalation is a function of the life-cycle of a conflict. Linear and cyclical models of conflict are useful simplifications of its complexity.

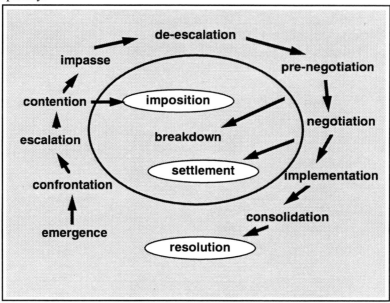

Figure 4: Dynamic Protraction Model of Conflict
Source: Mitchell (1993)

Chris Mitchell presents a dynamic protraction model of conflict, which represents it as a potentially cyclical process:

> protracted conflicts can pass through a wide variety of stages in their "life cycle". Moreover, this progression may not be linear, in the sense that some conflicts circle back to "earlier" stages and might pass through both malign and benign cycles of interaction several times.[38]

One possible sequence of stages is presented here (Figure 4). The idea of stages of conflict escalation and de-escalation is well developed. For example, Friedrich Glasl proposed a nine-stage model of conflict escalation for use in industrial disputes.[39] These models show that the third party role varies according to the stage of de-escalation. Third parties can sometimes impose a settlement, but in the case of protracted social conflict, this is likely to break down as soon as the third party is no longer in a position to impose its will. Third parties can help belligerents move beyond an impasse by providing assurances and incentives. Providing channels of communication and verifying information facilitates prenegotiation and helps prevent breakdown in negotiation. Assurances, incentives, and supervision help with the final stages of implementation and consolidation.

Hugo Prein illustrates how third party approaches can be guided by an understanding of the stage of escalation a conflict has reached. He finds from experimental settings that consultation is more effective when miscommunication and mistrust are high while mediation is more successful when a desire to resolve substantive issues is central.[40]

The Contingency Model of De-escalation

The contingency model of third party intervention suggests simply that there are different third party intervention activities appropriate to different stages of a conflict. Ron Fisher developed this concept to illustrate the importance of peacebuilding as a stage in the de-escalation process that can eventually lead to resolution of a conflict.[41]

The contingency model of third party intervention suggests that effective intervention is contingent upon the context of the conflict, the characteristics of the belligerents, the nature of the conflict, the intervention strategy, and the desired outcome.[42]

Fetherston's Model

The most comprehensive application of conflict resolution theory to the problem of peacekeeping is found in Betts Fetherston's paper Toward a Theory of UN Peacekeeping. She builds on Bercovitch's work on international mediation,[43] Deihl's critique of peacekeeping,[44] Fisher's work, and her own study of the evolution of peacekeeping. The result is a perceptive linkage of the practical business of peacekeeping with the promise of eventual resolution offered by a contingency theory of intervention. Within this framework, Fetherston suggests three roles for peacekeepers:

> First is the role of conflict control which provides the base level of activity of peacekeeping preceding the application of either of the other two roles. Second is the facilitation of an atmosphere conducive to negotiations and settlement, and in the long term movement toward

resolution. Third is the facilitation of an actual settlement and resolution process.[45]

Fetherston links the stages of the peacekeeping process[46] at two levels. She describes the macro level as the realm of states, the UN, and diplomats, and the micro level as the level at which peacekeepers interact with the combatants.[47] In military terms, her macro level corresponds to the strategic level, and her micro level to the tactical level. This omits the operational level, at which strategic ends are interpreted and resources are mobilized and applied to achieve them.[48] Fetherston's framework can be combined with Ron Fisher's scheme for de-escalation and the traditional military distinction between tactical, operational and strategic levels to yield a useful model of the role of peacekeepers in de-escalation.

A De-escalation Model for Peacekeeping

The timing of the works cited above is not coincidental. They reflect a fundamental change in the nature and objectives of peacekeeping brought about by the end of the Cold War. The change is twofold. First, local conflicts are no longer eclipsed by the pervasive threat of escalation to conflict between the superpowers—a threat which often obscured the true nature of the conflicts for on-lookers in the East and West, if not for the participants.[49] Second, there is a corresponding opportunity to make real progress towards the resolution of protracted social conflicts, thus making the world a safer and more humane place. Simply put, since 1989 the UN has used peacekeeping forces to intervene in conflict with the hope of moving that conflict towards a solution. Even long-standing missions like Cyprus, which once stood as mute testimony to the fact that progress was optional (perhaps not even desirable) are now under pressure to move forward to a settlement or drop off the list of conflicts demanding the attention of peacekeepers.

The new status of peacekeeping was made explicit in the recent UN review and subsequent declaration on peacekeeping operations:

> peacekeeping operations are in essence a temporary measure designed to promote the settlement of conflicts and disputes . . . [they] should never be a substitute for the ultimate goal—the speedy settlement of the conflict through negotiations...[50]

This means that peacekeeping can properly be seen as part of the spectrum that runs from high-intensity conflict to just and stable peace, with the legitimate aim of all security forces being to move away from the former, towards the latter, while safeguarding the interests of their constituencies (local interests in the case of the opposing forces, and international stability in the case of third parties intervening in the conflict). In other words, peacekeepers prior to 1989 were concerned primarily with keeping the lid on a conflict, or preserving the *status quo.*[51] Since 1989, the expectation has been that conflict will move towards settlement, and peacekeepers are therefore part of a process that helps to *de-escalate* the conflict. This spectrum is illustrated in Figure 5.

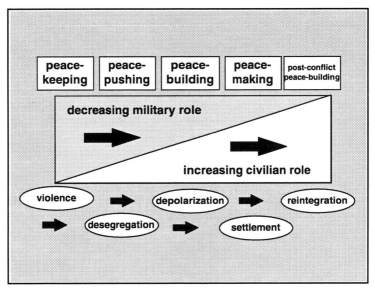

Figure 5: Spectrum of Conflict De-escalation

What Third Parties Do to De-escalate at the Operational Level

The spectrum of conflict de-escalation describes five stages. First, the fighting must be stopped, usually entailing separation of combatants. Second, the combatants must be pushed towards settling their disputes non-violently. Third, trust and confidence must be established to permit resolution. Fourth, the conflict is resolved (hopefully). Finally, the conditions which gave rise to the conflict are altered to prevent reversion to violence.

The model above suggests that, as the conflict de-escalates, military roles decrease, with a corresponding increase in the other instruments of influence (diplomatic, economic, and informational). It is probably also true that the balance of military and nonmilitary roles shifts as one moves from the tactical and operational to the strategic level of analysis.

Stopping the Fighting

The first stage in conflict resolution is to achieve a cessation of hostilities and provide some assurance that the cease-fire will continue. The ease with which a cessation of hostilities can be attained depends on the nature and origins of the conflict and the means which are available to end it. Mitchell identifies three elements to the structure of conflicts: a conflict situation, conflict behaviour, and conflict attitudes.[52] Particularly when a conflict situation arises from incompatible values *and* incompatible goals, it may be simultaneously reinforced by the conflict attitudes and behaviour of groups and individuals acting autonomously (violence from the bottom up) and decision makers directing events (violence from the top down).[53] This combination, which exists now in Yugoslavia, Lebanon, and several former Soviet Republics is particularly resistant to solution. It has encouraged some to advocate forcible separation of parties, the making of a cease-fire, or in some lexicons (erroneously) "peace-making."[54]

The Secretary-General has defined peace-making as a diplomatic activity: ". . . action to bring hostile parties to agreement, essentially through such peaceful means as those foreseen in Chapter VI of the Charter of the United Nations."[55] This is in keeping with earlier views of the distinction between military and diplomatic roles,[56] but is at odds with the more interventionist mood of today.[57] If a cease-fire is achieved through force, the intervening force must then be withdrawn and replaced with a neutral body which meets the prerequisites for a peacekeeping force. Neutrality and acceptability to both sides are essential if peacekeepers are to employ contact skills, but are unlikely to be present in the wake of forceful imposition of a settlement. The cessation of *legitimate* hostilities (those sanctioned by the authorities to whom military forces respond) marks the dividing line between war (to the left of the spectrum in Figure 1) and peacekeeping, which the spectrum illustrates. Violence can continue after this point, and the preeminence of the military role is directly proportional to actual and potential violence inherent in the situation. UN forces repeatedly failed to enforce cease-fires agreed at the political level in Bosnia and Croatia; conventional military force may be necessary to stifle violence at the tactical level, even when representatives of the belligerents have agreed to a cease-fire. This is the sort of mission now being referred to as "peace enforcement" by some, relying more on Article 40 of Chapter VII than Article 36 of Chapter VI.

The idea of deploying military forces early to prevent the spread or intensification of conflict is an old one, built into the Charter of the United Nations in both Chapters VI and VII. Inis Claude describes the limited practice of these functions as they evolved during the Cold War: "The only significant military function which might reasonably be attributed to the UN is that suggested by the theory of preventive diplomacy—the theory of operations, analogous to UNEF and ONUC, designed to assist the great powers in keeping the Cold War cold."[58]

The official UN definition of peacekeeping emphasizes lack of enforcement powers on behalf of the peacekeeping force: " . . . an operation involving military personnel, but without enforcement powers, established by the United Nations to help maintain or restore peace in areas of conflict."[59] These definitions encompass those other activities to the right of peacekeeping in the spectrum of conflict de-escalation and resolution. All of these start from the intervention of an international third party with the consent of the parties to the conflict.

Peace-Pushing

When the fighting has stopped, and sometimes even before, third parties need to assist in bringing the parties to the conflict to the table.

"Peace-pushing" is a term used by Ron Fisher in his work on third party intervention.[60] When third parties have sufficiently high stakes in a conflict, and sufficient influence, they may offer incentives or impose sanctions on parties to drag them to the negotiating table.

Peace-pushing at the strategic level must overcome barriers to negotiations, such as reluctance to move first, exaggerated perceptions of hostility, and the setting of conditions. Indirect diplomacy, the use of third parties, cautious overtures, and talks about talks are all means of overcoming reluctance to negotiate an end to hostilities.[61] International actions like sanctions, blockades and embargoes are indirect means of influencing leaders at best, but have an even more uncertain impact on the propensity for violence from the bottom up. Bilateral incentives, guarantees or the freezing of assets sometimes have a greater impact, but again have an uncertain impact on the armed man in the attic who hates his neighbour.

If it follows a cease-fire, peace-pushing at the strategic level may rely heavily on the peacekeeper to hold the line at the operational and tactical levels, against both organized forces and the man in the attic. At the same time, sanctions imposed by the United Nations may generate hostility towards the peacekeeping force, making it more difficult and more dangerous for them to hold the line.

Peace-Building

"Peace-building" has been used recently by Boutros-Ghali to describe the activities which occur after a settlement (peace-making) to prevent the recurrence of conflict.[62] Ron Fisher has also argued that it is a necessary step between peacekeeping and peace-making—building the trust and confidence necessary to negotiate in good faith and arrive at lasting solutions.[63] Documents of the Conference on Security and Cooperation in Europe (CSCE) also refer to peace-building measures, such as notification and observation of exercises, declarations of military holdings, doctrine seminars, and other confidence-building measures.[64] All of these are relevant to protracted social conflicts and might be instituted between belligerents either directly or with the assistance of a third party.

Although conceived at the strategic level, CSCE initiatives have practical application at the operational level. Professional military contacts at the working staff level have been deliberately sponsored as a vehicle for mutual understanding and tension reduction.[65]

At the tactical level, peace-building normally occurs between each side and the UN, as the force establishes trust and confidence in its mandate. More rarely, the force may be able to act as a lubricant between the conflicting interests of opposing communities, permitting peace-building between the communities and the militias representing them.

The idea that understanding can contribute to a broader peace process hinges on the belief that interests are not fundamentally inimical. If third parties can foster this belief, they advance the cause of peace-building, whether it occurs at the tactical, operational, or strategic levels.

Peace-Making

Peace-making in the traditional sense of a diplomatic solution might be divided into two stages: "settlement," in which the situation is stabilized, but the sources of conflict remain; and "resolution" in which the conflict has been terminated with little risk of recurrence. These are illustrated above in Mitchell's model (Figure 4). In a strict sense, peace-making does not occur at the operational or tactical levels, but only at the strategic level.

In a broader sense, however, any solution to a local conflict that prevents recurrence might be viewed as tactical "peace-making." If belligerents reach an agreement in a sector or theatre which reconciles opposing interests, it might be labelled a settlement. For example an agreement to disagree about the exact location of a cease-fire line or the extent of a buffer zone might be regarded as a settlement, and the process leading to it as an operational example of peace-making. However, peace-making at this level should not be confused with the ultimate objective of the peacekeeping force. The extent to which such local settlements serve to hinder or advance the broader cause of peace is uncertain.[66]

Post-Conflict Peace-Building

Finally, in the aftermath of a conflict, to prevent its recurrence, the international community and the parties to the conflict themselves must engage in post-conflict peace-building: "Peacebuilding is a positive, continuous, cooperative human endeavour to build bridges between conflicting nations and groups. It aims to enhance understanding and communication and dispel the "wandering rocks" of distrust, fear and hate."[67]

Instruments of Third Party Intervention at Operational Level

It is at theatre level in the office of the Special Representative of the Secretary-General (SRSG) and the force headquarters that the military instrument is given operational direction in pursuit of strategic aims. If the aims are diffuse and the strategy unclear, the military instrument is unlikely to be directed effectively. The same is true for coordination of economic measures, information, and diplomatic activity.

At the operational level, military peacekeeping forces are just one of the instruments available to third parties to assist in the control and de-escalation of violent conflict. Diplomatic, economic, and informational instruments have been alluded to above, but bear repeating in the specific context of the operational level.

Diplomatic/political influence is wielded directly by the SRSG and political officers. It is also wielded indirectly through national representatives and embassies, acting according to national interests. Non-national political influence might be attained by NGOs like the Carter Center, the American Friends Service Committee, or even academic groups working at intercommunal level in the conflict zone.

Information is one of the most powerful instruments of influence, though not one which is easy to control. People in the West are accustomed to thinking in terms of the power of CNN and the multinational media reporting primarily to an English-speaking world. At the operational level, the parties to the conflict may be largely impervious to the international media—influenced by their own media in their own language. The extent to which information tools can be mobilized and used to reach the belligerents is a major determinant of success in de-escalation. General Romeo Dallaire, Commander of UNAMIR in Rwanda in 1994, pleaded for a radio broadcast capability to counteract the effects of propaganda which were causing massive refugee movements in Rwanda.[68]

Economic instruments of third party intervention include all those activities and resources aimed at sustaining or improving life: aid, development assistance, humanitarian activities (health, welfare, and refugee activities) to name a few. When directed by state governments, some of these may be used for strategic purposes. For example, if a state provides refugee assistance directly to prevent immigration, it is using a strategic instrument; if it distances itself from the problem by contributing to a multinational effort coordinated by a third party, this effort is now at the operational level, subordinated to the strategic aims of the "international community." The distinction is important because national initiatives which serve national strategic interests may not be easily reconciled with multinational efforts in an operational theatre. This is true for each of the instruments of influence.

Each of these instruments can be used to influence the process of conflict de-escalation, but the focus here is on the contribution made by military forces. It is apparent that many of the functions of de-escalation referred to above lie outside the normal realm of military activity. The dividing line between military and nonmilitary responsibilities is not always clear, but it is clear that close coordination of military and civilian activities at the operational level is essential.

De-escalation Tasks at the Tactical Level

Having derived a spectrum of conflict de-escalation activities from the nature of protracted social conflict, conclusions about military activities must now be drawn. Fetherston distinguishes between military (or combat) and contact skills.

The first requirement of a peacekeeping force is to separate belligerents. This is a military task which requires combat skills discussed at length in Chapter Three. Even this task, however, must normally be conducted without recourse to coercion:

> The basic paradox of peacekeeping is the fact that it is a peaceful
> third party intervention but is often carried out on the ground by
> military personnel.[69]

The insight of Fetherston's statement is that the conceptual framework for peaceful third party intervention was developed without reference to armed force. The bridge between the third party role and the evolution of peacekeeping is the constabulary role of peacekeepers.[70]

Constabulary Intervention

Constabulary intervention occurs when soldiers of the peacekeeping force behave as a police force to halt or deter the actions of opposing forces. In its most basic form, it consists of a soldier standing in full view and dissuading hostile acts by word or gesture.

In the early stages of a typical conflict de-escalation cease-fire violations are still common. At platoon and company level, officers approach their counterparts and demand compliance. When a cease-fire is well established and shooting has become rare, shouting, rock throwing, and obscene gestures risk upsetting the fragile peace. These infractions can be dealt with by the "constable" on the beat— the private soldier or his section sergeant. The calm physical presence of a UN soldier between opposing forces, admonitions to each side, and the threat of calling upon the offender's superiors to discipline them has been effective in calming situations which could erupt in new violence. This sort of intervention is only effective after the cessation of hostilities.

When shooting has stopped and the segregation is effective, the presence of the blue-helmeted "police force" changes the norms of behaviour in the opposing forces. When an isolated shot does occur, the response is to lodge a complaint with the UN as one would to a civil police force, rather than to return fire.

The constabulary role can be carried further, once segregation has been effective and in place for a while. Shots can be treated as criminal matters, for resolution by the civilian police, reinforcing the norm that shots by either opposing force are not to be tolerated under the cease-fire. Soldiers on the scene act as policemen, maintaining a stable and orderly background against which combatants come to rely not on force of arms, but on recourse to the adjudication of a neutral third party.[71] This is the main impact of effective police practices in civil society, which rely on presence and assertion of a positive influence more than on coercion.[72] Constabulary intervention, then, is the classic tool of peacekeeping forces at the tactical level for maintaining a stable segregation of forces once an effective cease-fire is in place.

To be effective at the tactical level, persistent violations must be escalated and dealt with convincingly at the operational level. Sometimes simple policing must even be escalated to the strategic level, in order to maintain the integrity of the force. Constabulary intervention remains a "defensive" tactic; it assists in the prevention of violence, but contributes little to the resolution of the conflict.

Arbitration

Like constabulary intervention, arbitration is used to control situations which might turn violent. In arbitration, "an authoritative third party provides a binding judgment by considering the opposing positions and imposing a settlement."[73] Binding judgment means that the freedom of action of the opposing forces is reduced; this implies a greater degree of control by the peacekeepers. There is limited scope for arbitration at the tactical level, unless there is manifest willingness at the operational and strategic levels to support the judgement rendered. The cease-fire "imposed" on the Arabs and Israelis in the former Palestine on 15 July 1948, with the clear threat of enforcement under Chapter VII of the UN Charter might be viewed as arbitration at the strategic level.[74]

An example of "tactical arbitration" early in a conflict (when violence is high) illustrates the difficulty and danger of attempting to impose a binding judgment on soldiers, even when their governments may have agreed to a cease-fire. A heavy machine gun had been firing at an opposing force position, when a UN armoured personnel carrier was parked in its line of fire. The section commander dismounted to insist that the machine gun continue to refrain from firing, in accordance with the cease-fire agreement.[75] The choice of firing at the neutral UN or abiding by the cease-fire which he knows to be in effect may be a hard one for a soldier under stress. If UN forces retaliate, they immediately lose their privileged position, and the soldier's choice becomes very easy; he is fully justified in shooting at anyone who shoots at him. Even rumours that UN soldiers have fired on his side may be reason enough, given the generalizing nature of ethnic conflict.[76] Despite the obvious danger, and the limited scope (because opposing forces normally outgun the UN) if the UN can win this battle, imposing a binding judgement on individual soldiers and their commanders whenever the mandate is threatened, then they have won the "main defensive battle"—stabilizing the conflict by preventing forces from shooting at each other or moving across lines. They are then ready to move to the "offensive"—helping to change attitudes about the conflict and preparing the way for peaceful coexistence.

As the conflict becomes more stable, binding judgements at lower levels become easier. For example, encroachments into the buffer zone are a constant theme in partitioned Cyprus. When soldiers of the opposing force appear in the buffer zone (or prevent UN movement through part of the buffer zone) platoon, company, and battalion officers in succession will render "authoritative" judgments about the location of the cease-fire line. Once escalated to the operational level, headquarters staffs must attempt to determine why such violations are occurring. This raises the requirement for "consultation," addressed below.

Peacekeeping forces may also attempt "mediation with muscle" or "power mediation."[77] While not as coercive as arbitration, "power mediation" involves providing incentives and disincentives for the opposing forces, to persuade them as forcefully as possible to abide by the terms of a cease-fire. The sticks and carrots available at the tactical and operational level are very limited. In particular, military forces will almost always be outnumbered and outgunned. Big sticks and big carrots, usually economic and diplomatic, exist only at the strategic level, and it is to this level which force headquarters must resort if violations are persistent.

At tactical and operational levels, the "power" of peacekeepers is derived from two sources: the degree to which they can be useful and the degree to which they can hamper opposing force goals. In the Canadian sector in Croatia, civil projects, such as rebuilding roads, restoring electrical power, and providing emergency medical treatment and medical evacuation, were all used as incentives to gain the cooperation of local civil and military authorities. In Cyprus, local control over electricity or water supplies has sometimes been used as a lever. Such levers must be used sparingly, as parties to a conflict will take extraordinary measures to evade pressure they consider unreasonable. These examples highlight the importance of an all-arms team, including engineers and signallers, and also the inter-relationship of peacekeeping and socioeconomic reconstruction.

Arbitration, then, is a technique which relies on a strong third party, hence support and firm direction from the highest levels. It is also essential at the tactical level, though difficult and dangerous, to win the first crucial battle to enforce a cease-fire. The problems inherent in arbitration illustrate a general principle: the greater the control the third party attempts to exercise, the more important the integration of strategic, operational, and tactical levels of peacekeeping.

"Go-between" Mediation

A third party mediator in a civil dispute normally acts in the presence of both sides at the same time, holding three-party meetings. This has rarely happened in peacekeeping missions, particularly at the tactical and operational level, because the focus has been on segregation of opposing forces. Segregation allows mistrust and lack of communication to turn relatively innocent acts by either side into threatening gestures. Acting as a "go-between," a UN officer can prevent misinterpretation of opposing force intentions and reduce the tension and hostility which might arise if each side were left to its own devices.

By insisting that it is notified of movements or exercises near a buffer zone, a peacekeeping force is able to provide reassurances that increased activity levels which can be observed by the other side are "normal," and that there is no imminent threat to the status quo. Sensitivity to the security concerns of each side is essential in fulfilling this function. UN forces must not be seen by either side as spies for the opposing force. At the operational level, a decision may be made to try to negotiate voluntary exchanges of information as a confidence-building measure rather than provide reassurances from the UN force.

The "go-between" role can help to preserve stability and enhance confidence in the segregation of forces. A measure of progress is the regularity with which the go-between model develops into true three-party mediation in a congenial atmosphere. It may be unrealistic to expect contact at the tactical or operational levels, especially between soldiers, until routine contact is established at the strategic level. Indeed firm political direction, or at least acquiescence, from the highest levels is a prerequisite for opposing force contact, whenever a military hierarchy exists. Insistence on contact between the military forces at least at operational level would allow effective mediation of disputes and the development of substantive confidence building measures.

In theory, then, mediation is an activity which may start out with the go-between function—a series of meetings with first one side, then the other. It generally begins at the strategic level, often in the form of the UN appointed mediator,[78] and is taken up at the operational and tactical levels to deal with specific problems. Once the situation has been stabilized, an impetus is needed from the strategic level to insist on direct contact at lower levels. This contact should allow the peacekeeping force to assist the opposing forces to develop their own solutions to security problems. Working together under UN supervision to solve specific disputes should reinforce norms of cooperation and common interest which existed prior to the conflict.

Conciliation

Conciliation by peacekeeping forces consists of actions and discussions to reduce the hostility each opposing force feels towards the other. In the process, conciliation erodes negative stereotypes which characterize conflict. It occurs at every level, and can be particularly effective at the tactical level, where platoon commanders of the UN force may meet with comparatively inexperienced opposing force company commanders who are prepared to believe the worst of their opponents.

The most common incidents at platoon and company level involve lack of discipline and minor infractions of the status quo. When one side complains of overmanning by the other (when an OP has more soldiers in it than permitted by local arrangement), the UN officer may point to similar infractions by the plaintiff's side. By pointing out that these acts are unintentional rather than part of a sinister plan, officers are encouraged to view their opponents as the mirror image of themselves. The peacekeeper, between both sides, is in a good position to reinforce empathy and undermine the negative stereotypes each side holds of the other.

When real rather than imagined violations occur, it is sometimes necessary to take action to demonstrate that the violation has been terminated. Decisive action by the UN can alleviate hostility directed at both the opposing force for violating the status quo and the UN force for allowing the violation to occur. Several examples can be found in the close quarters of the old city of Nicosia, Cyprus, where visibility is restricted and ignorance feeds suspicions.

Although conciliation is an important tool, it is strictly limited by a posture of armed confrontation between the opposing forces. When there is a cease-fire but no peace accord initiatives at the tactical and operational level more ambitious than those mentioned above should probably be confined to civilians; higher commanders will actively sponsor suspicion of the other side. Anything other than low-key conciliation by peacekeeping forces may be regarded as subversive and can only be effective in the peace-building or post-conflict peace-building stages.

This raises the issue of conciliation between the civilian populations, which must start early in the peace-building process. Peter Loizos has described the pathology of hatred which can lead to inter-communal killing. Key factors are: the selective history taught by nationalists; the example of nation-state behaviour; local ideas of will, power, domination, and revenge; and the logic of ethnic conflict as collectivist and nonspecific—"us" against "them"—which absolves the perpetrator of responsibility for his actions and makes any of "them" a legitimate target in atonement for the sins of their countrymen. Since these factors are culturally determined they could be expected to vary from one conflict to another, underlining the importance of cultural sensitivity for any officer engaged in conflict resolution.[79] While these factors develop in youth, they come to maturity in the serving militiamen.

The need to target education as part of a comprehensive strategy of reconciliation is acknowledged in the Secretary-General's "Set of Ideas on an Overall Framework Agreement on Cyprus."[80] This is just one of many points at which civilian agencies and the peacekeeping forces need to coordinate their activities. The militarily-controlled buffer zone can serve as a bridge rather than a barrier between the two communities: the annual UNFICYP spring fair (held since the 1980s until reductions precluded it in 1993) saw thousands of Greek and Turkish Cypriot civilians mingle in the United Nations Protected Area. Following this precedent it would make sense to run joint school tours of the buffer zone rather than the current nationally sponsored bus tours on each side which reinforce negative images of the community on the other side.

Socialization of young men in military service solidifies inter-communal conflict. In post-war Germany, the allies established the *zentrum innere fuhrung* or "centre for inner leadership" to provide liberal democratic political education to the officers of the post-war German army, combatting the effects of wartime socialization and any tendency toward militarism. With the consent of the communities involved, supervision of officer education and militia training could provide an analogous basis for conciliation. Professional armies are also in a position to provide the incentive of high quality training assistance, on the condition that opposing forces participate jointly. Adventure training in small mixed groups of the sort encouraged at the United World Colleges is an ideal vehicle for developing a new generation of military leaders.[81] This sort of initiative belongs in the post-conflict peace-building phase and requires sophisticated techniques of education and socialization which may be perceived as invasive.

Confidence-building measures (CBMs) should also be considered as a means of reducing hostility, although they can also be considered a separate activity. Under the CSCE formula, CBMs were negotiated multi-laterally, but a third party intervening in conflict has the option of negotiating information measures or supervising challenge inspections or verification. Effective confidence building measures would certainly contribute to actions and discussions reducing hostility.

Conciliation, then, has applications at the operational and tactical levels during the segregation phase, but not much can be expected of it. Later in the conflict resolution process, initiatives at the strategic level might allow its introduction through confidence building measures or training and education programmes.

"Principled Negotiation"

The term "principled negotiation" comes from the Harvard Negotiation Project, which was a multidisciplinary effort to develop effective strategies for conflict resolution. Fisher and Ury offer three criteria for judging the effectiveness of negotiations: they should produce agreements which serve the legitimate interests of both parties; they should be efficient; and they should improve, or at least not damage the relationship between the parties. There are four basic tenets of "principled negotiation": separate people from the problem (do not make it a conflict of personalities); focus on interests, not positions; invent options for mutual gain; and insist on using objective criteria for evaluation.[82] There are critics of principled negotiation who claim that it is inappropriate where there are fundamental value incompatibilities—not everything is negotiable. There are also practical guides to negotiation which omit mention of principle and focus on the marketplace techniques of haggling—cooperative and confrontational.[83] Between these two extremes, the Harvard Negotiation Project offers concrete guidelines for appropriate negotiating behaviour to achieve the goals of the peacekeeping force. It is a good starting point to develop negotiating skills in officers.

As is evident from the examples Fisher and Ury offer, the technique is applicable to every level at which negotiations occur. The difficulty for the peacekeeper is to determine the objectives of the negotiation, and the best alternative to a negotiated agreement, or BATNA. He cannot do this in isolation, and must have concrete guidance from the next level up about the aims of his negotiations.

"Principled negotiation" is a technique applicable at any level, throughout the conflict resolution process, but it is a two-edged sword. Like any technique relying on local initiative, the strategic and operational goals, the UN aims and interests, must be clearly spelled out so that negotiators are consistently pushing in the same direction. Without this, opposing forces seem to cynically bide their time when faced with a "hard" negotiator, knowing that a "soft" one will come along eventually.

The distinction between hard and soft negotiators is sometimes mistaken for another distinction—that between distributive and integrative approaches to a negotiating (or bargaining) situation.

Distributive and Integrative Negotiations

Distributive negotiations deal with opposing interests, usually concerning allocation. Negotiations over territory, the location of cease-fire lines, access to resources and so on are distributive; more for one side is generally less for the other.[84] A "hard" bargainer is sometimes seen as one who will yield little and aim to gain much, sometimes using coercive or underhanded tactics.[85] Arbitration and mediation in a commercial setting attempt to find gains for each side, but the outcome is normally distributive. Integrative negotiations, on the other hand, address interests and the roots of conflict. Using techniques like Eiseman's "integrative framework construction" building on each parties "theories in use," incompatible positions can sometimes be reconciled.[86] Consultation[87] and problem-solving workshops[88] are other integrative techniques which provide a vehicle for altering perceptions and attitudes in order to arrive at a solution which does not violate the fundamental interests of either party. Those who do not understand integrative negotiating techniques sometimes mistake these for "soft" approaches. This is a particular risk in military cultures.

Problem-Solving Workshops and Consultation

All the techniques above deal with the UN and one party. There are practical reasons that unit officers, and even headquarters staff, have limited ability to engage in three-party encounters, even if these were to become easy to arrange as the result of a strategic breakthrough.

When officers of the UN force begin to deal with both sides in the same meeting, the need for well-developed contact skills increases dramatically. In a simple two-party meeting at company or battalion level, the use of a translator keeps the pace slow and reduces the scope for complex discussions. With amateur translators (usually young privates or corporals from the opposing forces) problems sometimes arise with translation of past and future tenses and limited vocabulary. Turning the meeting into a three-way, three language affair would require intense preparation and rehearsal, just to overcome these simple frictions. There is also the potential for explosive confrontations, verbal and even physical, when opposing forces are brought together.

Careful preparation, the adroit use of social occasions, and selection of participants based on detailed knowledge can all be used to mitigate these difficulties. However, it is almost certainly beyond the capacity of combat arms officers at unit level to overcome all of these problems in the space of a six-month tour. Three-party encounters are therefore probably the preserve of specialist teams of staff officers and civilian advisors at the operational level. At the operational level, problem-solving workshops and consultation might be considered.

Problem-solving workshops could follow the guidelines outlined in Fetherston,[89] drawing on mid-ranking staff officers for participants. The focus of such a workshop would be concrete security measures of advantage to both sides. For example, problems of movement control across the buffer zone, supervision of civilian activity in the buffer zone, and notification of exercise activities near the buffer zone might be subjects for discussion.

Initially, it is unlikely that workshops could have more than an exploratory role, but with time they could develop an advisory role, and might eventually be entrusted with limited decision-making authority on routine matters. The key to their success would be arriving at creative and mutually beneficial solutions to common security problems. Even if they never achieved this level of utility, problem-solving discussions conducted in the right atmosphere between professional soldiers at the operational level, with the assistance of UN military facilitators, could be a useful precursor to negotiations conducted at the strategic level.[90] Problem-solving workshops are more than an academic concept; they have been used in Cyprus by Ron Fisher, and Canadian officers have attended several inter-communal meetings. Although there is some scepticism about the extent of their potential, these workshops have made some progress in identifying mutual and opposing interests.[91] It is arguable that professional officers entering such discussions are doing so with greater commonality between their respective cultures and interests than are civilians attempting the same process.

Defensive and Offensive Tactics

In a mission where violent conflict is the enemy, defensive tactics stem its tide, and offensive tactics attack the mistrust and fear which feed it. Table 4 illustrates the relationship between combat and contact skills used for offensive and defensive peace operations, as suggested by theory.

Table 4: Tactics Derived from Theory

	"defensive" tactics	"offensive" tactics
combat skills	self defence constabulary skills	N/A
contact skills	arbitration negotiation go-between	mediation conciliation problem-solving consultation

Summary and Conclusions

This chapter has sought to derive from conflict theory a range of things which might be done by peacekeepers to de-escalate and control violence.

Theory which is relevant to intergroup conflict in general, and to protracted social conflict in particular should be the basis for assessing peacekeeping tasks, because these conflicts present the greatest challenge to peacekeepers at the tactical and operational level. The nature of violence which peacekeepers face will be addressed in greater detail in Chapter Three and Chapter Four.

Building on Sandole's categorization of the causes of conflict, the following conclusions are drawn about functions which a third party should attempt to sponsor. There is a requirement for physical separation, particularly in the most violent stages of conflict. Education and incentives to adjust attitudes and beliefs must be incorporated in the campaign plan. Basic needs, particularly for security and identity, must be met for all parties. The intervening force should not be perceived as catering primarily to the needs of one side. The effects of structural violence and rank disequilibrium should be identified and countered explicitly. Confidence-building measures should be initiated to counter negative self-fulfilling prophecies and hostility spirals. External pressure should be used to derail conflict processes, with the intervening force offering guarantees to each side.

Many of these appear to be functions for the strategic level, rather than battalion and force headquarters operating at the tactical and operational levels. Yet tasks at every level are related to these functions, for both civilian and military efforts to control and de-escalate violence.

At the operational level, the military arm of third party intervention, represented by the force commander and the civilian arm represented by the SRSG must cooperate in the following tasks: separation of combatant forces, without severing communications; bringing the parties together; building trust and confidence; problem-solving and reconciliation; and post-conflict reconstruction.

At the tactical level, tasks and techniques derived from theory include: combat skills related to the constabulary role; defensive and force-protection measures; force posture in conjunction with negotiations; contact skills related to both offensive and defensive operations; bargaining and distributive negotiations; and problem-solving and integrative negotiations. In the next chapter, the tasks associated with conflict de-escalation will be further identified by drawing on military doctrine and experience.

Endnotes

1   Parts of the material in this chapter were included in a paper presented to the Biennial Conference of the Inter-University Seminar on Armed Forces and Society held in Baltimore, MD, 22-24 September 1993.

2   International Peace Academy, Peacekeeper's Handbook (New York: Pergamon, 1974), 25.

3   Hans J. Morgenthau, Politics Among Nations: The Struggle for Power and Peace, 5th ed., rev. (New York: Knopf, 1978).

4   Kenneth N. Waltz, Theory of International Politics (Reading, MA: Addison-Wesley, 1979); F.H. Hinsley, Power and the Pursuit of Peace: Theory and Practice in the History of Relations Between States (Cambridge: Cambridge University Press, 1965).

5   Michael Howard, The Lessons of History (London: Yale University Press, 1991), 176.

6   Edward E. Azar, "Protracted International Conflicts," International Conflict Resolution: Theory and Practice (Sussex: Wheatsheaf, 1986), 28-39.

7   Stephen C. Lonergen and David B. Brooks, The Economic, Ecological and Geopolitical Dimensions of Water in Israel (Victoria: Centre for Sustainable Regional Development, 1993), 9.

8   Thomas F. Homer-Dixon, "On the Threshold: Environmental Changes as Causes of Acute Conflict," International Security, (Fall 1991), 76-116.

9   Robert D. Kaplan, "The Coming Anarchy" The Atlantic Monthly, 273:2 February 1994, 44-76.

10 Astri Suhrke, "Pressure Points: Environmental Degradation, Migration and Conflict," Occasional Paper of the Project on Environmental Change and Acute Conflict, no. 3, March 1993.

11 Nazli Choucri and Robert North, Nations in Conflict: National Growth and International Violence (San Francisco: W. H. Freeman and Sons, 1975).

12 David Elder distinguishes between ethnic separatists, political insurgents seeking to replace a government and those simply seeking change to existing government without seeking to replace it. These distinctions are useful because they have a bearing on the sort of tactics third parties might adopt.

13 Istvan Kende, "Twenty Five Years of Local Wars," Journal of Peace Research, (1990), 5-22.

14 Lincoln P. Bloomfield and Allen Moulton, CASCON III: Computer Aided System for Analysis of Local Conflicts User Manual Beta Test Version 2.0 preliminary version, (Cambridge, MA: MIT Center for International Studies) unpublished with Addendum 7, dated 7 January 1991.

15 Patrick Brogan, The Fighting Never Stopped: A Comprehensive Guide to World Conflict Since 1945 (New York: Vintage Books, 1990).

16 Ted Robert Gurr, Minorities at Risk: A Global View of Ethnopolitical Conflicts (Washington, DC: United States Institute of Peace Press, 1993), 314-315.

17 Ibid., 316.

18 J. W. Burton Global Conflict: The Domestic Sources of International crises (Brighton: Wheatsheaf, 1984), 19.

19 John Paul Scott, Aggression (Chicago: University of Chicago Press, 1958), 126.

20 A. Bandura Aggression: A Social Learning Analysis (Englewood Cliffs, NJ: Prentiss-Hall, 1973).

21 Arthur Koestler, The Ghost in the Machine, (New York: Macmillan, 1967), 234-255.

22 Peter Loizos, "Intercommunal Killing in Cyprus," Man, 23 (1988), 639-653. Since these factors are culturally determined they could be expected to vary from one conflict to another, underlining the importance of cultural sensitivity for any officer engaged in conflict resolution.

23 Dennis J. Sandole, "Paradigms, Theories and Metaphors in Conflict and Conflict Resolution: Coherence or Confusion?" in Conflict Resolution Theory and Practice, Integration and Application, eds. Dennis J.D. Sandole and Hugo van der Merwe (New York: Manchester University Press, 1993) 11.

24 Leon Festinger, A Theory of Cognitive Dissonance (Stanford, CA: Stanford University Press, 1962).

25 J. Dollard, L.W. Doob, N.E. Miller, O.H. Mowrer, and R.R. Sears, Frustration and Aggression (New Haven, CT: Yale University Press, 1939).

26 J. Galtung, "A Structural Theory of Aggression," Journal of Peace Research, 1 (1964): 167-191.

27 A.H. Maslow, Motivation and Personality (New York: Harper and Row, 1987).

28 Galtung, op. cit.

29 J.C. Davies. "The J-Curve of Rising and Declining Satisfactions as a Cause of Some Great Revolutions and a Contained Rebellion," in Violence in America: Historical and Comparative Perspectives, eds. H. D. Graham and T. R. Gurr (New York: Bantam Books, 1969); J.C. Davies, When Men Revolt and Why: A Reader in Political Violence and Revolution. (New York: Free Press, 1971).

30 Sandole, op. cit. 15.

31 Burton, op. cit. 6-7.

32 Vamik Volkan, "The Need to Have Enemies and Allies: A Developmental Approach," Political Psychology, vol. 6 (1985), 219-245; and The Need to Have Enemies and Allies: From Clinical Practice to International Relationships (Northvale, NJ: Jason Aronson, 1987) by the same author.

33 Gurr, op. cit., 87.

34 Robert Jervis, Perception and Misperception in International Politics (Princeton, NJ: Princeton University Press, 1976), especially Chapter 3.

35 Jim Wall and Rhonda Callister, "Conflict and its Management," (unpublished paper, 1994), 13.

36 Ibid., Table 3, 63. The authorities for each of the causes identified are discussed in pages 17-23.

37 Ibid.

38 Christopher R. Mitchell, "Problem-solving exercises and theories of conflict resolution," in Conflict Resolution Theory and Practice: Integration and Application edited by Dennis J. D. Sandole and Hugo van der Merwe (New York: Manchester University Press, 1994), 87.

39 Friedrich Glasl, (1982) "The Process of Conflict Escalation and Roles of Third Parties," 119-140 in Conflict Management and Industrial Relations edited by Gerald B. J. Bomers and Richard B. Preston, (Boston, MA: Kluwer-Nijhoff Publishing).

40 Hugo Prein, "A Contingency Approach for Conflict Intervention," Group and Organization Studies, 9:1 (March 1984) 81-102.

41 Ronald J. Fisher, "The Potential for Peacebuilding: Forging a Bridge from Peacekeeping to Peacemaking," Peace and Change 18, (1993,) 247-263.

42 Jacob Bercovitch, "International Mediation: A Study of the Incidence, Strategies and Conditions of Successful Outcomes," Cooperation and Conflict, 21:3 (September 1986) 155-168.

43 Ibid.; Jacob Bercovitch, Social Conflict and Third Parties: Strategies of Conflict Resolution. (Boulder, Co: Westview 1984); Jacob Bercovitch, "Third Parties in Conflict Management: The Structure and Conditions of Effective Mediation in International Relations," International Journal, 60:4 (Autumn 1985), 737-752; J. Bercovitch, Theodore Anagnoson and Donnette L. Wille, "Some Conceptual Issues and Empirical Trends in the Study of Successful Mediation in International Relations," Journal of Peace Research, 28:1 (February 1991) 7-18; and Jacob Bercovitch and Jeffrey Z. Rubin, eds, International Mediation: A Multi-Level Approach to Conflict Management. (London: Macmillan, 1991).

44 Paul F. Diehl, "When Peacekeeping Does Not Lead to Peace: Some Notes on Conflict Resolution," Bulletin of Peace Proposals 18:1 (1987) 47-53 and "Peacekeeping Operations and the Quest for Peace," Political Science Quarterly, 103:3 (Fall 1988), 485-507 by the same author.

45 A. B. Fetherston, Toward a Theory of United Nations Peacekeeping, Department of Peace Studies, University of Bradford, Peace Research Report Number 31, (February 1963), 60-61.

46 Following Boutros-Ghali's Agenda for Peace, Ms. Fetherston has labelled these peacekeeping, (with the current UN definition) peacemaking (meaning diplomatic settlement) and peacebuilding (meaning steps to alter conditions to prevent a recurrence of conflict).

47 Fetherston, op. cit., 36-38.

48 It is perhaps the omission of the operational level from her analysis which leads her to the observation that reserve peacekeepers are more appropriate than regular soldiers who have been trained to use force, citing several authorities (79-80). Harleman, Mackinlay and Beattie, all with military experience, are talking about soldiers working at the tactical level. They are not

talking about units, formations, or staffs being employed at the operational level as part of a campaign plan. This is a crucial difference, and none of the above would deny the contribution which professional military expertise must make to the operational, as opposed to the tactical level.

49 Seymour M. Finger, "The Maintenance of Peace," Proceedings of the Academy of Political Science, 2:4 (1977), 195-205.

50 Ehab Fawzy, Rapporteur, "Comprehensive Review of the Whole Question of Peace-Keeping Operations in all their Aspects," Report of the Special Committee on Peace-Keeping Operations. Draft, A/47/92-23222 3101c (E), 1 June 1992.

51 The Blue Helmets: A Review of United Nations Peacekeeping, (New York: United Nations Department of Public Information, 1985), 8. This lists seven peacekeeping forces which were launched between 1956 and 1978 and six observer missions.

52 C. R. Mitchell, The Structure of International Conflict, (London: MacMillan, 1981), 15-34.

53 There is insufficient space here to develop the argument that the spectrum of conflict resolution rests on the nature of the conflict structures and attributes. Conflicts with different attributes require different approaches to resolution.

54 This term caused a great deal of confusion when it appeared in a draft US manual, FM 100-20 Operations Other Than War in 1989. The US definition is now congruent with international usage (See FM 100-23 Peace Operations final draft, Chapter 2, and FM 100-20 Operations Other than War, initial draft, 3-2).

55 Boutros Boutros-Ghali, Agenda for Peace, (New York: United Nations, 1992), 11.

56 I. J. Rikhye, M. Harbottle, and B. Egge, The Thin Blue Line: International Peacekeeping and Its Future, (New Haven, CT: Yale University Press, 1974).

57 My own view is that this use of the term muddies the water a great deal; either a peace is "made" by consensus, or it is not. If it is not, the international community has recourse to force under Chapter VII of the UN Charter. The idea that you can shoot your way to a settlement à la "peacemaker" missiles and the Colt "peacemaker" is a peculiarly American idea.

58 Inis L. Claude, "United Nations Use of Military Force," Journal of Conflict Resolution, 7:2 (June 1963), 117.

59 The Blue Helmets, op. cit., 3.

60 Ronald J. Fisher, "The Potential for Peacebuilding: Forging a Bridge from Peacekeeping to Peacemaking." Unpublished paper, 1992; Ronald J. Fisher and Loraleigh Keashly, "The Potential Complementarity of Mediation and Consultation within a Contingency Model of Third Party Intervention," Journal of Peace Research, vol. 28, no.1 (February 1991), 29-42.

61 Paul R. Pillar, Negotiating Peace: War Termination as a Bargaining Process (Princeton, NJ: Princeton University Press, 1983), 78-86.

62 Boutros-Ghali, op. cit., 11.

63 Fisher, op. cit.

64 CSCE, Charter of Paris for a New Europe, (1990); CSCE, Peaceful Settlement of Disputes (Annex 3) Berlin Meeting of the CSCE Council, 19-20 June 1991, (1991); CSCE, Prague Document on the Further Development of CSCE Institutions and Structures CSCE Second Meeting of the Council, Prague 1992, (1992).

65 Opening remarks at the first Seminar on Military Doctrines and Strategies, held in Vienna, January 1990; CSCE, Report of the CSCE Meeting of Experts on Peaceful Settlement of Disputes, Valetta 1991, (1991).

66 Diehl, "When Peacekeeping Does Not Lead to Peace," 47-53.

67 Fetherston, op. cit., 41, citing the International Conference on Peacebuilding (1986) Summary of Proceedings.

68 Major-General Romeo Dallaire and Ambassador Passage speaking at the CGSC/USAWC International Peace Operations Conference, 18-20 October 1994.

69 Fetherston, op. cit., 77.

70 Much has already been written on this subject, including William J. Durch, ed., The Evolution of UN Peacekeeping: Case Studies and Comparative Analysis (London: St. Martin's Press, 1993); and N. D. White. The United Nations and the Maintenance of International Peace and Security (New York: Manchester University Press, 1990).

71 Michael N. Harbottle, The Impartial Soldier, (London: Oxford University Press, 1970).

72 M. Bard and J.Zacker, The Police and Interpersonal Conflict: Third-Party Intervention Approaches. (Washington: Police Foundation, 1976).

73 Fisher, op. cit., 13.

74 The Blue Helmets, op. cit., 18.

75 This is an apocryphal story; it may have happened in 1974, but I have found no documentary evidence. It is provided as an illustration only.

76 Loizos, op. cit., 639-653.

77 Fisher, op. cit., 14.

78 The Blue Helmets, op. cit., 13 (Arab-Israeli conflict), and 262 (Cyprus).

79 Loizos, op. cit.

80 UN S/2472 21 Aug 1992, 23: "A bi-communal committee will be established to review the text books used in schools on each side and make recommendations for the removal of material that is contrary to the promotion of goodwill and close relations between the two communities. The committee may also recommend positive measures to promote that objective."

81 It must be emphasised that mutual understanding and respect at the junior leader level has a small impact on violence from the bottom up, and none at all on violence from the top down. There are stories from Yugoslavia of officers, formerly professional colleagues and friends, caught on either side of the civil war. The investment in junior leaders may take 30 years to pay dividends.

82 Roger Fisher, William Ury, and Bruce Patton, Getting to Yes: Negotiating Agreement Without Giving In, 2d ed., (Harmondsworth: Penguin, 1991).

83 Leonard Koren and Peter Goodman, The Haggler's Handbook: One Hour to Negotiating Power (New York: Norton, 1991).

84 Ibid.

85 Ibid. The authors define their haggling tactics as cooperative, coercive, and neutral.

86 Jeffrey W. Eiseman, "Reconciling 'Incompatible' positions," The Journal of Applied Behavioural Science, 14:2, (1978), 133-150.

87 R. J. Fisher, and Loraleigh Keashly, "Third Party Interventions in Intergroup Conflict: Consultation is Not Mediation," Negotiation Journal, 4:4, (October, 1988), 381-393.

88 A. B. Fetherston, "The Problem Solving Workshop in Conflict Resolution," Peacemaking in a Troubled World, edited by Tom Woodhouse (New York: Berg, 1991), 247-265.

89 Ibid.

90 Ronald J. Fisher, "Prenegotiation Problem-Solving Discussions: Enhancing the Potential for Successful Negotiation," International Journal, 44, (Spring 1989), 442-474.

91 Costas Apostolides, "Peace-building in Cyprus," The Cyprus Mail, (5 September 1993).

Chapter Three

Peacekeeping Doctrine and De-Escalation

Chapter Two deduced from theory a range of roles and tasks for the control and de-escalation of violence in protracted social conflicts. This chapter extends those roles and tasks by examining military peacekeeping doctrine. In the framework presented in Chapter One, doctrine is related to theory through principles and yields tactics, techniques, and procedures. This chapter deduces from doctrine and theory the range of military tactics and techniques which might be used by peacekeepers to handle violent incidents.

Sources of Doctrine

Within NATO, doctrine consists of "fundamental principles by which the military forces guide their actions in support of objectives. It is authoritative but requires judgement in application."[1] More generally, it is a statement of how to conduct operations and how to think about operations. It provides the common base from which tactics, techniques, and procedures can be developed to deal with specific circumstances.[2]

In conventional war-fighting doctrine, it would be unusual to find a doctrine manual which attempted to cover every aspect of war-fighting from the decision to embark on war and the mechanism for assembling coalitions to techniques for constructing trenches and conducting patrols (and incidentally, omitting any mention of campaign planning). Yet this was the state of peacekeeping doctrine until very recently. It is not a reflection on the authors of doctrine, but rather on the status of peace operations (or any "operation other than war") as somehow peripheral to the business of soldiers.

In the last four or five years, a more consistent approach to peacekeeping doctrine has been taken, with manuals tending to focus either at the top end, on policy and concepts or on the application of techniques in field operations. Table 5 lists the official sources consulted for this study, and identifies their focus. It should be noted that some of these manuals are still in draft form, and it is likely to

Source:	Concept and Policy	Staff Procedure	Field Operations
UN Training Guidelines for National or Regional Training Programmes (1991)	♦		
UN Guideline: Standard Operating Procedures for Peace-Keeping Operations (1992)	♦		
UN Peace-keeping Handbook for Junior Ranks (Draft) (1994)			
UK FM Wider Peacekeeping (Second Draft) (1994)	♦		
UK FM Volume V: All Arms Tactics, Special Operations and Techniques, Part 1. Peacekeeping Operations (1989)		♦	♦
Nordic UN Tactical Manual, Volume 1 (1992)	♦	♦	
Nordic UN Tactical Manual, Volume 2 (1992)			♦
Canadian Forces Publication 301-3: Peacekeeping Operations (1992)	♦	♦	♦
UN Peacekeeping Operations: Organization, conduct and logistics functional duties of personnel (Russian handbook) (1993)		♦	♦
Russian-United States Guide for Tactics, Techniques and Procedures of Peacekeeping Forces during the Conduct of Exercises (1994)			♦
US Joint Pub 3.07-3: Joint Tactics, Techniques and Procedures for Peacekeeping	♦	♦	
US FM 100-23: Peace Operations (1994)	♦	♦	

Table 5: Sources of Doctrine

be many years before doctrine for peace operations matures to the level of doctrine for conventional combat.

The state of peace operations doctrine has two implications for the handling of violent incidents. To the extent that doctrine reflects experience, it simply describes how armies do business now. Since there are few examples of operational success, doctrine is likely to be a weak guide to the operational art of de-escalation. On the other hand, new and unfamiliar circumstances create an opportunity for doctrine to evolve based on theory, which in turn can shape practice at the operational or tactical level. This is the pattern William DePuy sought to establish for American doctrine in 1976.[3]

Peacekeeping Principles

As the link between theory and doctrine, principles distill lessons of theory, which in turn is a generalization of experience. Principles are fundamental elements. They are important for the way military organizations learn because they serve as guidelines for action, and embody fundamental constructs of military thought.[4] The principles which have been espoused for peacekeeping are one starting point for tactics, techniques, and procedures developed to handle violent incidents.

A consideration of principles is one of several possible starting points as thinking about peacekeeping has not always been well integrated with relevant theory. In the absence of a clear conceptualization of peacekeeping as a form of third-party intervention, principles have been derived directly from experience. The consequences of this can be seen in some of the differences in peacekeeping principles adopted by countries with and without much peacekeeping experience.

Comparative Peacekeeping Principles

The most important of the principles are the ones most widely accepted, because they represent the greatest commonality of experience. These are impartiality of the force, consent of the belligerents, minimum use of force, and clarity of purpose.

The divergence of American principles reflects the American interpretation of peacekeeping as one of a number of "operations other than war" (OOTW). Although the American peacekeeping manual cites OOTW principles as applicable to peace operations,[5] it also refers to many of the more widely held principles as dimensions of peace operations (section 3-1). Interestingly, a recent American guide to tactics, techniques, and procedures for low intensity conflict lists principles of peacekeeping which coincide almost exactly with UN and UK principles.[6]

Significant differences in principles are worth noting because they indicate different points of departure for doctrine, and suggest that different tactics, techniques, and procedures might emerge for handling violent incidents. In this case, one might expect American forces to react more readily than some with use of force when faced with a violent situation; however, "principles" are only one of many factors at work, and seldom dominate training.

Clarity of Intent

The Nordic manual states that "It is essential that both sides are made fully aware of what the peacekeeping forces are trying to achieve and why."[7] This applies at every level, for large and small operations. The corresponding British principle is transparency: "Consistent with the requirements for operational security, the parties to a conflict in a Wider Peacekeeping environment should be made as fully aware as possible of the motive, mission, and intentions of the UN force."[8] Canadian doctrine focuses clarity at the operational and strategic level, referring to the importance of a clear and enforceable mandate: "The role and tasks for the force must be clearly worded, defined, understood and agreed to."[9]

What is not explicit in doctrine is that long-term and short-term intents can conflict at the tactical level. In a confrontation, is it the peacekeepers' intent to resolve the immediate situation, or seek a longer-term solution? A short-term solution to confrontation might entail coercion; a frustrated convoy commander may be able to force his way past a check-point, or a patrol may have the strength to seize weapons in a restricted area. These actions may be within the letter and spirit of the force mandate at the time and place of execution, but may not contribute to the longer term intent of seeking a peaceful resolution to the conflict. In fact, they may lead to a cycle of escalating shows of force or violence: one day a convoy forces its way past a checkpoint, the next it is shot upon, a stronger escort is provided and so on. On the other hand, failing to demonstrate resolve may produce a weak and harassed peacekeeping force which is not taken seriously by the belligerents and fails to inspire confidence. This might be the problem underlying UNPROFOR's woes in Bosnia:

> Bosnian Serbs hijacked five truckloads of international medical supplies yesterday in an ominous new assault on the United Nations relief mission in Bosnia, UN officials said. . . . Renewed Serb-Muslim fighting and Serb blockades and harassment of UN aid operations are making a mockery of the UN security zone around Sarajevo.[10]

The principles of "consent" and "minimum use of force" provide the answer to the dilemma of conflicting intents at the tactical and operational level. When the legitimate authorities governing the warring factions consent to the specific mandate of the peacekeeping force, reasonable actions in support of that mandate are legitimate, whether taken by the peacekeeping force, observers, staff, or the belligerents themselves. More sensitivity surrounds use of force than non-coercive actions which might be taken.

Use of Force

The use of force has two faces in peacekeeping doctrine. The first is minimum use of force, and the second is use of force for self-defence only. These are not synonymous. The first permits the use of force to achieve objectives related to the military mission, while the second restricts use of force to reaction to threats to person or property. The doctrinal approach to use of force has changed over time. This is in part because the circumstances of the first 13 peacekeeping missions were different from those which have been launched since the end of the Cold War.

Following the setbacks to UN forces in the Congo (ONUC), there was a lot of discussion of the need for self-defence, and the ways in which use of force by UN forces should be limited.[11] Kjell Goldmann, writing for the International Information Centre on Peace-keeping Operations shortly after ONUC, illustrated self-defence concepts ranging from narrow to broad, based on six questions. This is shown in Table 6.

Table 6: Self-Defence and Use of Force

Question	Narrow	Conditional	Broad
Can active tasks be undertaken against possible resistance, without the prior consent of all parties?	No	Only when there is little risk of armed resistance, though consent is not necessary	Yes
Is escalation of force permissable?	No	Some escalation is permissable	Yes
Is anticipation or preemption permissable?	No	Preemption is, but prevention is not	Yes
Can obstacles to freedom of movement be removed forcibly?	No	Only if obstacles threaten the security of the UN force	Yes
Can a military victory be exploited for bargaining purposes?	No	Only in order to increase UN security	Yes
May force be used *after* violence is done to UN personnel?	No	Only in order to liberate captives	Yes

Goldmann and others writing after him point out that a broad interpretation of self-defence is tantamount to permitting enforcement of the mandate, even when the operation is authorized under Chapter VI rather than Chapter VII: "Allowing a force to take positive action in defence of its purposes is no different from allowing it to enforce them."[12] Writing with the benefit of 25 years more hindsight than Goldmann, White also argues that this is absolutely necessary for a peacekeeping force to be effective in a civil conflict: "To deny it [a peacekeeping force] *de facto* enforcement powers is to render it ineffective for the purposes of fulfilling its mandate."[13] By 1992, even the Secretary-General seemed to be having doubts about the absolute requirement for consent and use of force in self-defence only. His Agenda for Peace refers to peacekeeping as an activity " . . . *hitherto* with the consent of all the parties concerned," (emphasis added) acknowledging that with the advent of missions to failed states, there would be parties to the conflict who had not given their consent.[14] Nevertheless, active measures on a small scale at the tactical level, taken within the overall framework of a cease-fire to which legitimate authorities have agreed, remain qualitatively different from *enforcement operations* without the consent of authorities.

The increasing acceptance of the active use of force in peacekeeping missions can be explained in part by the changing context of peacekeeping missions. The first thirteen missions occurred against a background of decolonization as well as superpower confrontation. There was an active non-aligned movement in the General Assembly suspicious of Security Council members' motives for launching missions. Many UN members were anxious to avoid reinforcing the structural violence of North-South domination and colonial conflict. The theme is evident in the language of the General Assembly, and explicit in many peace research publications.[15]

With an eye on structural violence, the International Peace Academy (IPA) explicitly linked consent and the use of force exclusively for self-defence in the Peacekeeper's Handbook. First, forces are not deployed except at the request or with the consent of the belligerent parties.[16] Second, force is not used to obtain an end to fighting, nor to maintain law and order. The authors cite the historical failure of military means to achieve a political solution:

> History shows how inconclusive have been the majority of enforcement actions in this [intrastate and community] category of conflict. Even where the weight of the military machine has crushed the militant opposition it has not succeeded in achieving a solution to the problem that created the conflict in the first place.[17]

The IPA acknowledges the risk of a peaceful intervention becoming counterproductive by merely reinforcing the status quo, but maintains that peaceful intervention has a greater chance of success than the use of force. The Peacekeeper's Handbook offers the most stringent limitation on the use of force:

> All UN operations have been based on the premise that peaceful and not enforcement methods will be used to achieve solutions in conflict and violence situations. A peacekeeping soldier may use his weapon only in defence of his life or in conjunction with his fellow soldiers to defend UN positions and/or property against attack. Such action is only meant to be taken in event of physical attack and then only as a last resort; it is not for UN troops to initiate the action.[18]

Nordic countries, with a strong heritage of peace research and memories of ONUC, have only recently expanded the use of force beyond this and remain predisposed to a narrow interpretation. The Nordic Tactical Manual offers six circumstances in which armed force may be employed. Of these, only the fourth offers ready scope for broad interpretation.

1) If there is an immediate danger of being arrested or hijacked;

2) If there is an immediate danger of being disarmed by personnel;

3) If armed forces are enclosing UN units;

4) If, by the use of force, armed forces try to prevent UN units from carrying out their mission;

5) When it becomes necessary to support UN units being attacked;

6) In the event of armed forces/personnel trying to take UN property, positions, vehicles, etc.[19]

British and French forces, with a history of imperial policing and a strong heritage of internal security operations to support the established order, have a broader interpretation of permissible use of force. Richard Smith describes a 1963 pamphlet, Keeping the Peace, in which the principle of minimum force is described: "no more force must be used than is absolutely necessary to achieve the immediate military aim."[20] Smith points out that this is a more expansive interpretation of the appropriate use of force than is permitted by purely defensive rules of engagement. Force can be used proactively, but each individual act must be legally justifiable, and must contribute to the maintenance of order. Punitive use of force was not sanctioned.[21]

Faced with the difficulties of peacekeeping in the Balkans, Britain may be returning to this earlier approach, after only recently publishing guidelines for traditional peacekeeping. The British manual, Peacekeeping Operations, published in 1988, distinguishes between active and passive force, based on the operating procedures of several long-standing missions (UNFICYP, UNDOF, UNIFIL, and the MFO):

> The passive use of force involves the employment of physical means which are aimed not to harm individuals, installation and equipment. . . . The active use of force involves the employment of means which result in physical harm to individuals, installations and equipment.[22]

It goes on to state that "Active force may only be used as a last resort in self-defence,"[23] taking the traditional line. The new manual, Wider Peacekeeping, addresses the use of force in the context of consent and impartiality.

> The misuse of force risks destabilizing peacekeeping operations and causing an uncontrolled and violent transition to peace enforcement. . . . The identification of the critical consent divide allows use of force to be addressed in a way that takes full account of its wider connotations. The need to preserve overall consent does not foreclose the use of force by peacekeepers. Indeed, majority consent may serve to marginalize a minority withholding consent and render it vulnerable to the use of force. If a strong consensual framework reduces the status of armed opposition to that of maverick banditry, then demonstrably reasonable and proportionate force may be employed against it without fear of fracturing the consent divide. . . . The principle of impartiality will also offer guidance on whether and how force might be employed. . . . Wider Peacekeeping doctrine

emphasizes that the consequences of using force reach far beyond the immediate tactical situation [emphasis in original].[24]

The new British "Wider Peacekeeping" doctrine permits initiation rather than merely active use of force in self-defence. The use of force must be proportional, must contribute to the accomplishment of the mandate in the longer term, must be applied impartially, and must be employed with the broad consent of a majority of the significant parties. Above all, the long term impact of the use of force must be considered. This last is particularly difficult for the commander on the ground faced with a series of violent situations.

American doctrine is the most liberal in its interpretation of the permissible use of force. FM 100-23 provides an accurate description of the dynamics of the interplay between consent, impartiality and the use of force, illustrated in Figure 6.

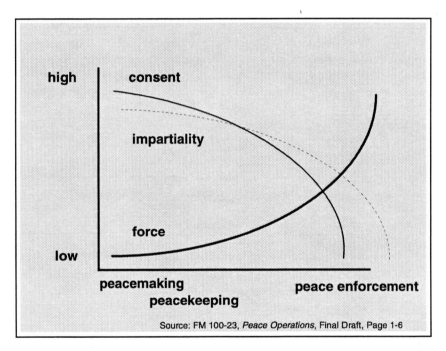

Source: FM 100-23, *Peace Operations*, Final Draft, Page 1-6

Figure 6: American View of the Peace Operations Environment

There is room to interpret this relationship as a *prescription* for the use of force, even though use of force may have negative consequences:

> The need to employ force may begin a cycle of increasing violence; therefore, the commanders must be judicious in employing forceful measures and must understand the relationship between force and the desired end state. Of the three variables, the level of force is

usually the only one over which the commander can exert dominant influence. Operational level commanders or higher authorities will usually decide about the use of force in this context (other than self-defence).[25]

To be accurate, the commander can exert dominant influence only over the level of force used by his own troops, not those of the belligerents. There is, of course, a direct relationship between force used by the third party and that used by belligerents for *increasing* levels of force, but not necessarily for decreasing levels of force; escalation is easier than de-escalation:

> The use of force to attain a short-term tactical success could lead to a long-term strategic failure. The use of force may attract a response in kind, heighten tension, polarize public opinion against the operation and participants, foreclose negotiating opportunities, prejudice the perceived impartiality of the peace operation force, and escalate the overall level of violence. Its inappropriate use may embroil a peace operation force in a harmful long-term conflict that is counterproductive to the overall campaign objective.[26]

The American manual goes on to say that in peacekeeping operations, use of force should be regarded as a last resort, and that it should be used with restraint in peace enforcement missions. The inherent right of self-defence applies as for other nations' doctrine, but a view which sets American doctrine apart from other interpretations is the statement that:

> In either case [peacekeeping or peace enforcement], sufficient force must be available to achieve objectives rapidly through simultaneous application of combat power.[27]

The emphasis on applying combat power to achieve objectives rapidly is at odds with the understanding of UN, British, and Canadian doctrine that peacekeeping missions do not achieve their objectives through the application of combat power, but through negotiations and that success will rarely be speedy. It is also at odds with the principle of "perseverance" found in American doctrine for operations other than war. That principle is compatible with the slow building of trust and confidence over time, and the resolution of conflict with the consent of the parties rather than through the application of combat power.

The direction in which Western doctrine appears to be moving is to accept the active use of force (intended to harm personnel, equipment or installations) in limited circumstances, while recognizing that it will often be counter-productive in the long run. Richard Smith describes a spectrum of willingness to use force in peace operations, which is illustrated in Figure 7. As noted above the British manual Wider Peacekeeping provides the most lucid explanation of when force can be effectively used in peacekeeping missions, and when this use becomes "peace enforcement" (indistinguishable from war). The crucial distinction rests in impartiality and consent.

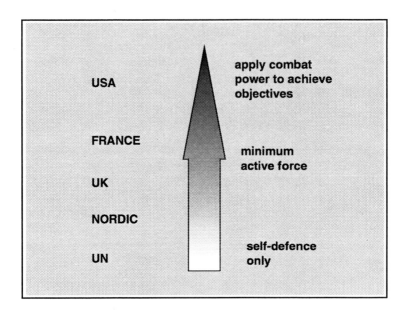

*Figure 7: Comparative Approaches to Use of Force
in Peace Operations*

Impartiality and consent

The principles of impartiality and consent are related because one is commonly perceived as a prerequisite for the other; a necessary but not a sufficient condition. Only when a belligerent is satisfied that a third party will consider every incident impartially on its merits is he likely to consent to intervention.

The Nordic UN Tactical Manual emphasizes impartiality and fairness as a basis for negotiations:

> Total impartiality and neutrality are essential in order to retain the trust and confidence of the parties to the dispute and of the host government. If and when a peacekeeping force is suspected of favouring one of the parties concerned, the other party will no longer trust the peacekeeping force. Once mutual trust has evaporated, the UN force will find it difficult to implement its mandate.[28]

Charles Dobbie, the author of Wider Peacekeeping has written that it is consent which distinguishes between peacekeeping and peace enforcement: peacekeeping depends on "a modicum of in-theatre consent"; peace enforcement "dispenses with consent and is conducted . . . in accordance with standard military principles predicated on the identification of an enemy."[29]

Dobbie's most significant contribution is in identifying the way in which consent at the operational level (the "modicum of in-theatre consent") actually facilitates active use of force at the tactical level to support the execution of the mandate. At the operational level (and above) consent derives mainly from formal agreements, and the boundaries of consent are fairly clear. At the tactical level, it is subject to many local influences, including the degree of control exerted by commanders. It will therefore vary according to time and place, causing conflict with the execution of third party functions. Dobbie argues that peacekeepers can use active force at the tactical level within the boundaries imposed by operational consent.[30] This concept implies that use of force is not only restrained and directed at "rogue elements," but constantly matched by liaison and negotiations to ensure that the boundary of consent is not breached. These efforts also provide incentives to belligerent commanders to maintain control of their forces. Figure 8 illustrates the way in which consent at the operational level separates peacekeeping from peace enforcement.

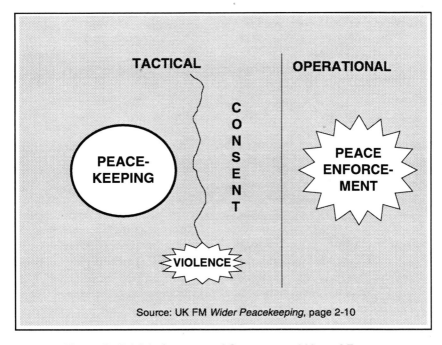

Source: UK FM *Wider Peacekeeping*, page 2-10

Figure 8: British Concept of Consent and Use of Force

According to Dobbie, consent is built on impartiality, legitimacy, mutual respect, minimum use of force, credibility, and transparency. It is undermined by taking sides, using too much force, loss of legitimacy, loss of credibility, disrespect, and misunderstanding.[31]

What is striking about this list of factors is the degree to which it is largely *independent* of combat effectiveness, but very much dependent on personal communications between the peacekeepers and the parties to the conflict.

One exception to this generalization is the use of minimum force. Strong and competent forces can assure their security and handle incidents more effectively, and are less likely to use force excessively. British doctrine expresses this with the phrase "maximum strength, minimum force," a lesson learned from their internal security type of operations.[32] Forces which can handle potentially violent situations without resort to violence are able to contribute to the preconditions for effective communications with the belligerents, building the consent required for effective peacekeeping--whether offensive or defensive.

Impartiality and consent are principles which permit a third party to minimize use of force effectively and maintain the aim or intent for which third parties are deployed.

What Do These Principles Mean for De-escalation Efforts?

Lanir argues that principles of war are transhistorical, and contain elements of contradiction—the dialectic inherent in war. The same is true for the principles of peacekeeping. Fetherston has pointed to the basic contradiction of military peacekeeping—between separating forces, and facilitating the reconciliation of the communities they represent.[33] In practice this contradiction is minimized when the operation is characterized by consent, impartiality and minimum use of force, which underscores the importance of these principles. Otherwise the contradiction is apparent between combat skills required for "self-defence," whether broadly or narrowly interpreted, and the contact skills used to reconcile differences.

Within these contradictions can be found the "mental constructs" which support offensive and defensive action in peacekeeping. Peacekeepers must be able to defend themselves against physical violence, and reduce the threat of violence over time. They must provide some assurance to each belligerent that the other will not transgress, and that transgressions will be dealt with when they are not deterred. These are "defensive" actions which rest on both the combat effectiveness of the intervening force, and its ability to maintain consent through personal contact with the belligerents at every level. The degree and pervasiveness of consent will influence the extent to which combat effectiveness is a prerequisite to any exploitation of personal contact by the third party.

In Chapter One, the "enemy" of a peacekeeper was defined as the conflict. By accepting this, a third party undertakes "offensive" action against the roots and causes of the conflict. This involves attempts to open communications and rebuild relationships between the communities. This offensive action rests on the personal connections and communications between the third party and the belligerents, and the eventual facilitation of direct contact between the belligerents. The degree and pervasiveness of consent becomes increasingly important, as personal contact becomes the main vehicle for offensive action. Combat effectiveness remains essential. Not only must security and confidence in the third party be maintained, but common military culture and respect for military capability will make military third party intervention more effective with military factions among the belligerents. Civilian third parties may have more success with civilian elements.

The principles of peacekeeping which have come to be widely accepted over the last forty years have implications for both military and civilian third parties intervening in a conflict. The most important is that long-term solutions are built on consent of belligerents, not on coercion. A corollary to this is that use of force by a third party has a defensive role, but not an offensive one. A second corollary is that inappropriate defensive tactics will hamper any subsequent offense.

Doctrine for Peacekeeping Tasks Related to Violent Incidents

The central role of consent is implicit in many, but not all, descriptions of peacekeeping tactics found in doctrine. It is more evident in discussions of personal contact skills than in those relying primarily on combat effectiveness.

Combat and Contact Tactics

Combat tactics are those in which basic military skills and physical force predominate. They include any situation in which there was a physical threat, weapons discharge, combat engagement, or internal security operation (cordon and search or crowd control, for example).

Contact tactics are those in which interpersonal communications and personal contact are dominant. They include exchange and liaison duties, interviews and public relations, negotiations or related discussions, civil-military cooperation, and inter-agency cooperation.

Fetherston distinguishes between these types of tactics because they have different purposes in the context of peacekeeping: "The military functions of peacekeeping are important and necessary, but the underlying *raison d'etre* of a peacekeeping force is the third party role . . . " which relies on contact skills.[34]

Both types of tactics are represented in peacekeeping manuals. Combat tactics are fairly consistently described, while manuals vary in their treatment of contact tactics. A third subject area treated in peacekeeping manuals might be described as generic military activities for any environment: driving, communications, first aid, field sanitation, and so on. Only combat and contact tactics will be discussed here.

Summary of Combat Tactics Prescribed by Doctrine

The United Nations Junior Ranks Handbook lists both individual and small group tasks which are likely to be required of peacekeepers. These include basic weapons-handling skills, counter-mine measures, field fortifications, patrols, convoy escort duties, and the establishment of observation posts.[35] It also includes a particularly useful, though superficial, section on de-escalation. "Demonstrations of masses" are met with crowd control; enduring ground violations are addressed by "tightening line procedures"; advancing troops are met with reinforcement of positions, blocking, tightening of area procedures; and constant sniping is addressed by interpositioning and show of force, and perhaps the deployment of reserves or "ready reaction groups." Although these are all combat tactics, the sketch of a "de-escalation deployment" shows the deployed forces linked by reports, liaison and negotiation to the opposing forces, and emphasizes that use of force is a last resort.[36] It is implied that incidents are de-escalated by combining deployment with negotiation, avoiding the use of force if possible.

The UN Training Guidelines list a series of collective combat tasks for which national contingents and staffs must prepare. These include the positioning and establishment of observation posts, mine-counter measures, positioning and management of check points, road blocks, and searches, patrolling, and training in the use of force. The guidelines demand that use of force be addressed for all levels in all modules, and suggest that it be dealt with in the following order: definition of force; when it can be used; principles for the application of force; how it is to be applied; authority for the use of force; and actions after force has been used.[37] The guidelines provide material on each of these topics, but leave room for interpretation by particular missions and national contingents. For example,

> The Force Commander may wish to reserve to himself the authorization to fire heavy support weapons (120mm Mortars) with authorization for the firing of other heavy weapons being reserved to the Battalion CO.[38]

The Nordic Tactical Manual provides information on use of force which parallels that of the training guidelines, discussed above. It has a detailed section on the conduct of interposition operations, including a number of different deployment patterns, and discusses riot control, response to hijacking, search operations, patrolling, roadside bombings and shootings, the handling of infiltrators, confiscation of weapons, and escort and guard duties. All of these are fairly standard "combat" tasks, but have different functions in the context of a peacekeeping mission.

Patrols, for example, have both a combat and contact element to them. They are intended to maintain observation, show presence, interpose or intervene, limit infiltration and provide for security of an area. They may also be required to investigate incidents, make contact with the local population, enhance confidence and collect information.[39]

The Nordic manual treats "tailing" under a separate heading. Drawn mainly from experience in UNTSO and UNIFIL, this is an operation in which a patrol follows a belligerent force to prevent violence against the civilian population and to protect private property. In this sort of operation, it is crucial to have communications with which to report or call for assistance. The idea is that a third party presence will restrain the actions of a belligerent, and help to protect the human rights of civilians. When a belligerent patrol enters a civilian dwelling:

> The object is to be followed into the building. Entry to the house must be made decisively, if necessary by pushing away personnel

blocking the entrance. Tailing men who are inside will follow the object and prevent violence to the people dwelling in the house, if necessary by interposing. . . Cameras are used openly and notes are made.[40]

Executing this sort of tactic clearly requires both the confidence of trained soldiers, and considerable interpersonal skill if violence is to be avoided while affording protection to the civilian party. In practice, what restrains the belligerent soldiers or militiamen (the "object" being tailed) is probably fear of retribution; by being observed, they are made accountable for their actions both to their own superiors and to the international community witnessing their actions through the UN force. The more explicit their accountability can be made through contact skills, the less requirement there is likely to be for combat skills. This is significant because it has direct parallels in the de-escalation campaigns examined in Chapter Five.

The British Field Manual, Peacekeeping Operations, addresses the same range of combat tactics as the Nordic Tactical Manual, and was used in its preparation.[41] The section on interpositioning provides more detail of the sort alluded to in both the UN Junior Ranks Handbook and the Nordic UN Tactical Manual: military operations aimed at interposition must be matched by liaison and negotiation at the appropriate level.

Stages in a typical deployment of an interposing force include: *preparatory work* in which the staff ensure that the force deployment conforms to the mandate and is acceptable to the parties; the *cease-fire agreement*, initially as a line on a map; *assessment of ability of the contestants to control their own forces*, and preparation by the force to meet "sporadic guerilla resistance" with defensive measures; *establishment of a liaison system*, prior to deployment, to enable deployment with consent and rectify misunderstandings; *deployment of peacekeepers in a buffer zone*, with the consent of the belligerents; *interpositioning to deal with lesser infringements* entails standing patrols, observation posts and use of armoured vehicles, concurrent with liaison and negotiation to remove the infringement; the occupation of the buffer zone is followed by detailed *delineation of demarcation, cease-fire and armistice lines and buffer zones*.[42] Once established and demarcated, the interposing force controls the line or zone using the same combination of combat and contact skills. The success of the interposition depends on combining effective military presence with effective communications to the belligerents.

A Russian peacekeeping manual, prepared in English, seems to draw on the UN training guidelines and several national publications. However it departs from earlier work, drawing on recent experience in Sarajevo to describe responses to specific incidents which link combat and contact tactics. The same pattern of linking combat and contact skills emerges in the Russian recommendations for handling sniper fire, shelling, opening fire, convoys halted at road blocks, and hijack attempts. The initial response to each of these events is defensive: get out of the line of fire, move to a shelter, ensure armed escorts at the front and rear of convoys, and so on.

Force can be used in self-defence, normally in the following sequence: verbal warnings if practicable; warning shots; aimed single shots on command; further warnings; fire for effect, returning fire with like fire; cease-fire and report.[43] When a reserve is deployed, it is done so for maximum effect on desire to negotiate:

> The aim is that the fast deployment of superior force to a point of confrontation or the location of an incident will defuse a situation and persuade the initiators of the action to back down and/or negotiate. . . . Almost always it will be more important for the protagonists to see the reserve deployed than for reserve to manoeuvre in a covert fashion.[44]

In each manual, some mention is made of the importance of linking these essentially military tasks to liaison, negotiation and the consent of the belligerents. Combat and contact skills, however, are not evenly treated.

Summary of Contact Tactics Prescribed by Doctrine

Contact tactics are neither as well developed nor as consistently addressed in peacekeeping doctrine as the combat tactics discussed above. In particular, techniques for conflict resolution such as problem-solving and consultation are not covered in any manual.

The UN Training Guidelines emphasize the connected tasks of negotiation, liaison, and investigation. In addition to these skills, the guidelines for the production of mission standard operating procedures include some details on the preparation of correspondence, handling of breaches of agreement, special meetings and hand-over procedures. While examples of *form* are given , there is little information on *content*. This would normally be provided by Force Commander's Guidelines or directives, which vary between theatres.

The Nordic UN Tactical Manual includes guidance on the importance of neutrality, reliability and impartiality as foundations for contact skills, on media relations, the negotiation system, use of liaison teams, cooperation with observers, good offices, and use of civilian police. The importance of UN leadership in building trust and confidence is emphasized with an extensive list of tips on behaviour.[45]

The Nordic manual also describes the escalating alternatives available to units faced with violations of the mandate. Negotiations and mediation are described as part of an escalating sequence consisting of: influence through negotiations and mediation; non-use of armed force by employing defensive means; and armed force.[46] The rationale presented is that, faced with a UN force negotiating, belligerents are most likely to negotiate and least likely to use armed force. Conversely, faced with use of arms, they are most likely to respond in kind and least likely to negotiate.[47] This reflects conflict research that suggests violence is likely to be a reciprocal, and often escalating, response.

The Nordic manual also offers the most detailed explanation of the sequence of escalation from negotiations to non-use of weapons to use of weapons. The chart presenting this is reproduced in Figure 9.[48]

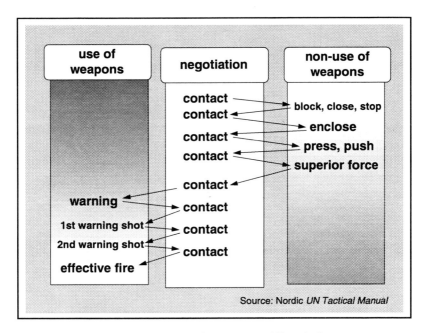

Figure 9: Nordic Sequence of Escalation

Several observations pertain to the nature of the contact. First, the subtle differences between "close," "enclose," and "press" are unlikely to be readily apparent unless reinforced by negotiation, underlining the importance of continuous contact during this escalation process.

Second, the degree to which local superiority of force can be achieved will influence the negotiation strategy. Third, the process is intended to slow down resort to effective (aimed) fire, and requires both restraint and military competence. Finally, the sequence is an escalatory one, and *de-escalation* is unlikely to occur in the same manner.

This process is alluded to in other manuals in less detail, sometimes leaving room for interpretation. In the manual developed for joint Russian-American peacekeeping exercises, for example, the possibility of sudden force is emphasized:

> Peacekeeping forces must always have the possibility to escalate step by step, or of breaking off the whole procedure. They should offer the opportunity for negotiation. *Activities may change rapidly from non-use of force to the use of force.* It is important that each counterpart has a possibility to react. Peacekeepers should remain alert for that possibility [emphasis added].[49]

The contact which occurs between a belligerent and the UN force is most likely to occur through the liaison system of unit officers and headquarters' staff officers attached to corresponding unit and formation headquarters. It may also rely on

UN Military Observers and even *ad hoc* liaison, particularly when irregular forces are involved.

The British Field manual addresses a similar list of subjects. Two main roles are identified for the liaison system, which may be more or less pervasive depending on the restrictions imposed by the belligerents and the UN Force: first, it attempts to settle disputes at a lower level; second, it provides for host government representation in the operational area. This can even extend to ambassadorial intervention on behalf of national contingents in some circumstances. Some uses of liaison officers include the conduct of inspections and investigations, accompaniment of the force reserve to avoid misunderstandings, interpreting and assisting at family meetings, and facilitating the movement of forces.[50]

Both the British and Canadian manuals provide good explanations of the "protest system" by which disputes are resolved at low level. Protests are made through the liaison system, or direct to counterparts. They are then investigated at an appropriate level, and meetings are held to resolve the disputes. What is not clear from doctrine is that the UN seldom acts as a "mediator"; most commonly, disputes arise between belligerents or between one party and the UN, and the UN negotiates on its own behalf or acts as a go-between. This is not just a technical detail, but profoundly affects the skills which are required by peacekeepers, and the tools available to them to resolve disputes. For example, if belligerents will not meet at low level under UN supervision, then a whole range of problem-solving and facilitating techniques are impracticable.

The draft Canadian manual offers an insight about the traditional distinction between the role of the military peacekeeper keeping the peace, and the diplomat's role to resolve the conflict:

> The purpose of incident reporting, registering complaints, and conducting investigations and negotiations is to reconcile the belligerents on a contentious issue or incident, so that conflict will not resume. The critical role of the peacekeeper is to reconcile problem areas and maintain the status quo, so that skilled diplomats, in a peaceful and constructive atmosphere, can work with the belligerents to resolve the conflict.[51]

The theory of conflict resolution discussed in the previous chapter suggests that the distinction of function is not as great as implied in this passage; the tactics of conflict resolution and de-escalation may be very closely related to the effectiveness of diplomatic strategies of conflict resolution.

The most widely accepted contact techniques for peacekeepers are liaison, investigation, and negotiation. Mediation and conciliation get a mention in some doctrinal publications, but without great emphasis. The other common thread in contact skills is their close link to combat effectiveness through the escalation process best described in the Nordic tactical manual.

Model of Contact and Combat Techniques at the Tactical Level

This brings us to the point of combining combat tactics and contact techniques at the tactical level. The first chapter listed 17 types of violent incidents which have faced peacekeepers. Soldiers and units equipped for peacekeeping missions are prepared to face these incidents with training and with orders. The incidents themselves involve belligerents with the capability (weapons, equipment, manpower) and intent to cause violence.

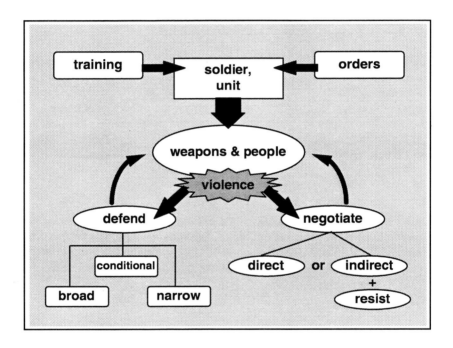

*Figure 10: Combat and Contact Techniques
at the Tactical Level*

Faced with a violent incident, peacekeepers can defend themselves and negotiate to resolve the incident. A general scheme of the options is illustrated in Figure 10. The extent to which active or proactive force is permitted by the mandate and force guidelines can be described according to Goldmann's description of narrow, conditional or broad interpretation of self-defence.

The potential to negotiate depends mainly on the type of incident. Often it will not be possible to enter into direct negotiations with the faction causing the incident: you cannot talk to snipers or mortar shells. When direct negotiations are not possible, the peacekeepers must take measures for self-defence and initiate indirect negotiations, relying on the liaison mechanism or established contacts with counterparts at higher levels of command.

There are at least three important conclusions from this scheme linking combat and contact techniques at the tactical level. First, self-defence targets primarily the effects of weapons, and even this is only a last resort. Peacekeepers normally defend against artillery and mortar fire, for example, with effective field fortifications, not counter-battery fire. Secondly, the will or intent of belligerents to use weapons offensively, rather than the weapons themselves, is the focus of contact with belligerents to handle a violent incident. This is related to the third conclusion: measures taken in self-defence should be calculated to enhance the bargaining position of negotiators rather than undermine them. For example, preventing a cut-off section from being disarmed and held hostage is likely to strengthen efforts to negotiate its release.

These conclusions do *not* suggest that peacekeepers must be militarily inert, relying only on talk and trenches to defend themselves. Rather they suggest that the way in which force is used by peacekeepers must be calculated to reduce the incentives of belligerents to use force, building on the principles of consent and impartiality. The insight of Charles Dobbie's Wider Peacekeeping is that judicious use of force at the tactical level can not only help to restore order, but can reinforce consent for the operation and assist in the de-escalation of violence.

Third Party Responses

The doctrine and principles reviewed in this chapter are derived from forty years of peacekeeping experience, and have been reviewed by hundreds of soldiers and staff officers with direct experience of the situations they address. From this doctrine, it is possible to deduce a range of tactics, techniques, and procedures with which peacekeepers can attempt to de-escalate violent incidents. When faced with a violent or potentially violent situation, what are the peacekeepers' options? As shown in Figure 10, they come down to talking and resisting.

Individual Responses

For the individual soldier, response to a violent incident is based on his military training and the orders he has received. The latter include but are not limited to the Rules of Engagement (ROE). Permissive rules of engagement might reflect Goldmann's broad or conditional interpretations of self-defence. Can or should the soldier fire if a weapon is pointed at him? Must he wait until the belligerent fires first?

Similar questions arise about the negotiating option. When can a soldier negotiate with a gunman? What can he offer? A common situation in Bosnia, for example, was the demand for "tribute" to pass a checkpoint. A corporal commanding a convoy would be threatened with violence and asked to donate food or fuel. What are the limits on direct negotiation, and how do these relate to the right of self-defence and the use of force in support of the mission?

Of course, many situations involving individual soldiers will not permit direct negotiations and can be addressed only by immediate defensive action and subsequent indirect negotiations. Table 7 illustrates the dilemma. Of the 17 types of violent incidents faced by soldiers, eight are not amenable to direct negotiations by the individuals involved. You cannot talk to a jet on a strafing run, nor to an unseen sniper. A further three may occur in circumstances which permit direct negotiations, but often will not.

Table 7: Individual Responses to Violent Situations

TYPE OF VIOLENT INCIDENT	DEFEND?	NEGOTIATE?
air attack	yes	no
air threat or demonstration	yes	no
indirect fire	yes	no
direct fire	yes	no
ambush	yes	no
sniper fire	yes	no
active mining	yes	no
drive by shooting	yes	no
physical attack on installation	yes	yes?
projectiles thrown	yes	yes?
moves forward in force	yes	yes?
unauthorized construction	no?	yes
restriction of movement	no?	yes
personal threat, intimidation	no?	yes
kidnapping or hostage-taking	no?	yes
riots or civilian violence	no?	yes

There are also at least six types of incidents which may occur in such a way as to preclude physical defence, leaving only negotiation as a means of controlling and de-escalating the situation. A three-man patrol surrounded by a company has little opportunity for self-defence; a mob may not listen to an emissary.

These general observations set the scene for examination of handling specific types of violence through a combination of defensive action, direct and indirect negotiation.

Collective Responses

Indirect negotiation is a collective response. When a soldier is pinned down by fire, his freedom to move is restored by suppressing his assailant from another point. This is the basis of fire and movement—one of the most basic collective skills taught to soldiers. "Defend and negotiate" is the peacekeeping equivalent of "fire and movement" at the tactical level. What is clear from a close reading of doctrine is that the "flanks" of the belligerents are their superiors. Whenever possible, the aim of the negotiation is to reinforce the control of the superior over the wayward subordinate. If the principle of consent applies at the operational level, then the pilot, observer, or sniper is not an enemy, but a misguided ally whose *intent* to use force against the opposing force or the third party must be changed.

The collective response to achieve this entails both adjusting defensive postures to remove incentives to violence, and negotiating to bring pressure to bear from superiors.

In cases where rogue factions are not under effective control, the same mechanisms of defence and negotiation apply to the collective response. The aim is to reduce the impact of the rogue faction on the larger de-escalation process, and bring the factions under effective control according to the agreement entered into by the belligerents. The primary responsibility for control of belligerent factions rests with the belligerents themselves, and the peacekeeper can expect to play only a supporting role in this.

Conclusion: The Range of Tactics

Peacekeeping doctrine has evolved to address basic military tactics such as patrolling, establishing positions, using force with restraint for self-defence, interposing forces and so on. It has linked these with contact skills and techniques which include liaison, investigation and negotiation in order to respond to incidents. From doctrine, a range of military tactics, techniques, and procedures can be deduced for use in controlling and de-escalating violent incidents. These can be summarized as follows. Individuals require contact skills to manage incidents in which they have the opportunity to negotiate directly. Corporals negotiating their way past militia checkpoints and soldiers on the verge of being kidnapped provide examples. Units require collective combat skills which can be used in relation to contact skills. Deployment of crowd control or the force reserve provide examples. Units and headquarters staffs also require collective contact skills to manage the deployment of forces and indirect negotiations. Use of the liaison system to bring pressure on sources of violence is an example. Finally, commanders and staff officers need individual contact skills to handle meetings, in which contact occurs. Subsequent chapters will examine the way in which these tactics, techniques, and procedures can be used at the operational and tactical levels to control and de-escalate violence.

Endnotes

1   JCS Pub 1-02, Department of Defense Dictionary of Military and Associated Terms, Incorporating the NATO Glossary of Terms and Definitions (English and French).

2   FM 100-5, Operations (Washington: Headquarters, Department of the Army, 14 June 1993), 11.

3   Major Paul H. Herbert, Deciding What has to be Done: General William E. DePuy and the 1976 Edition of FM 100-5, Operations, Leavenworth Papers, Number 16, (Fort Leavenworth: Combat Studies Institute, 1988), 1.

4   Zvi Lanir, "The 'Principles of War' and Military Thinking," Journal of Strategic Studies 16:1 (March 1993), 15.

5   FM 100-23, Peace Operations, Comprehensive Dummy, (Washington, D.C.: Headquarters, Department of the Army, 22 September 1994), 3-4.

6   CSM James J. Gallagher, Low Intensity Conflict: A Guide for Tactics, Techniques and Procedures (Harrisburg, PA: Stackpole Books, 1992), 110-111.

7   Colonel Johan Hederstedt, Lieutenant-Colonel Jorn Hee, Major Nils W. Orum, Major Simo Saari, and Captain Olli Viljaranta, Nordic UN Tactical Manual, Volume 1 (Jyvaskyla, Finland, 1992), 27.

8   Wider Peacekeeping, 2d draft, 3-17.

9   B-GL-301-303/FP-001, 1st draft, 1-8.

10   Reuter and Associated Press,"Bosnian Serbs Hijack Medical Supplies, Dangerous Showdown Develops as Troops Refuse to Leave Demilitarized Zone," Toronto Globe and Mail, (Tuesday, 18 October 1994), A2.

11   See, for example, Mona Harrington Gagnon, "Peace Forces and the Veto: The Relevance of Consent," International Organization 21:4 (Autumn 1967), 812-836, D.W. Bowett, United Nations Forces: A Legal Study (New York: Praeger, 1964), 231-232 which found that there was not a requirement for consent when fighting represented a threat to international peace, reflecting a broad interpretation of self-defence; Asbjorn Eide, "United Nations Forces in Domestic Conflicts," in Peace-Keeping: Experience and Evaluation - the Oslo Papers, ed. Per Frydenberg (Oslo: Norwegian Institute of International Affairs, 1964), 251-252, which suggests that use of force other than in self defence must be authorized under Articles 41 or 42 of the UN Charter.

12   N. D. White, The United Nations and the Maintenance of International Peace and Security (New York: Manchester University Press, 1990), 201.

13   Ibid., 209.

14   Boutros Boutros-Ghali, An Agenda for Peace: Preventive Diplomacy, Peacemaking and Peace-keeping, report of the Secretary-General pursuant to the statement adopted by the Summit Meeting of the Security Council on 31 January 1992, United Nations, New York, 11.

15   For example, Johan Galtung, "Three Approaches to Peace: Peacekeeping, Peacemaking and Peacebuilding," Impact of Science on Society, (1976).

16   International Peace Academy, Peacekeeper's Handbook (New York: Pergamon, 1974), 22.

17   Ibid., 23

18   International Peace Academy Peacekeeper's Handbook, 3d ed., (New York: Pergamon Press, 1984), 38. The section goes on to explain use of force by ONUC, which sometimes fell outside this definition.

19   Nordic UN Tactical Manual, Volume 1, op. cit., 32.

20   Richard Smith, "The Requirement for the United Nations to Develop an Internationally Recognized Doctrine for the Use of Force in Intra-state Conflict," Strategic and Combat Studies Institute, The Occasional, Number 10, (1994), 24 (quoting Keeping the Peace, vol. 1 (London: War Office, 1963), 2).

21   Ibid., 24.

22   UK Army Field Manual Volume V, All Arms Tactics, Special Operations and Techniques, Part 1: Peacekeeping Operations (London: Her Majesty's Stationary Office, 1988), 6-17.

23   Ibid., 6-19.

24 Ibid., 2-10 to 2-12.

25 Peace Operations, op.cit, 13.

26 Ibid., 33-34.

27 Ibid., 34.

28 Nordic Tactical Manual, Volume 1, op. cit., 27.

29 Charles Dobbie, "A Concept for Post-Cold War Peacekeeping," Survival, 36:3 (Autumn 1994), 121.

30 Ibid., 124-126.

31 Ibid., 132-133.

32 Wider Peacekeeping, op. cit.

33 A.B Fetherston, Toward a Theory of UN Peacekeeping, (Department of Peace Studies, University of Bradford, Peace Research Report No. 31, February 1993), 71.

34 Ibid., 77-78.

35 United Nations Department of Peacekeeping Operations Training Unit, Junior Ranks Handbook, (New York: DPKO, 1994).

36 Junior Ranks Handbook, op. cit., Section 6.

37 United Nations Training Guidelines for National or Regional Training Programme (New York: United Nations Department of Peacekeeping Operations, 1991), 50-54.

38 Ibid., 52.

39 Nordic Tactical Manual, Volume 1, op. cit., 39-43.

40 Ibid., 82-83.

41 Interview with Olli Viljaranta, January 1993.

42 Peacekeeping Operations, op. cit., 6-1 to 6-6.

43 Russian Peacekeeping Centre, UN Peacekeeping Operations: Organization, Conduct and Logistics, Functional Duties of Personnel (Moscow, 1994), 122-123.

44 Ibid.

45 Nordic Tactical Manual, Volume 1, op. cit., 39-43.

46 Ibid., 29.

47 Ibid., 30.

48 Ibid., 31.

49 US Foreign Military Studies Office, Russian-United States Guide for Tactics, Techniques and Procedures of Peacekeeping Forces During the Conduct of Exercises, (Fort Leavenworth, KS: Foreign Military Studies Office, 1994), 80.

50 Peacekeeping Operations, op. cit., 7-2 to 7-12.

51 Canadian Forces Publication, B-GL-301-303/FP-001 Peacekeeping Operations, 1st draft (Ottawa: Department of National Defence, 1992), 6-29.

Chapter Four

Combat and Contact Skills in Practice

Conflict resolution theory suggests that contact techniques such as negotiation can be used to control and de-escalate violent incidents. Some of these techniques are reflected in military doctrine for peacekeeping. Doctrine also describes the deployment and use of military forces to control situations. These have been referred to as combat or management techniques.[1] This chapter puts combat and contact techniques into the context of two recent missions for which survey data are available. Since the survey data leave gaps in our understanding of the role of soldiers, anecdotes from various missions have been included.

The aim is to link operational experience to the theory and doctrine reviewed in the previous chapters. Emphasis is on the experience of individual soldiers and officers. The conclusion specifies the ways in which contact and combat techniques are linked to handle specific incidents at the lowest tactical level. Experience reviewed in this chapter shows that units are capable of independent *defensive* action to stop belligerents shooting and moving against each other, but they cannot coordinate effectively *offensive* action to increase trust, confidence and interaction between communities. This insight introduces the requirement for integration of de-escalation efforts at unit and headquarters level and the development of campaign plans for peace operations which will be discussed in later chapters.

Data on Combat and Contact Experiences

There is surprisingly little accessible data on operational experience of peacekeeping missions. Various sociologists have examined some aspects of identification and correlates of performance and soldier support,[2] but few data have been collected on what peacekeepers actually do or how they do it.

Canadian Experience in Former Yugoslavia

The Peacekeeping Interview Program conducted by Dr. Ken Eyre for the Canadian Armed Forces consisted of three parts.[3] The first two parts included a yes/no survey questionnaire of 94 questions, and several open-ended questions. The third part consisted of 42 videotaped interviews with command appointments and individuals who had had significant experiences.

The surveys were administered to approximately 1,200 soldiers and officers of 5ième Groupe de Brigade who served in UNPROFOR. The 2ième battalion, Royal 22ième Régiment (R22eR) infantry served in the relatively static buffer zone mission, Sector West, in Croatia and the Serbian Krajina. The 12ième Régiment Blindé (12 RBC), an armoured unit, served in the much more fluid environment of convoy escort duties and support to humanitarian operations in Sector South, Bosnia. Both units served from November 1993 to April 1994.

The data sample has several shortcomings. First, the survey was completed after the unit returned to Canada, thus reserves and attachments who made up almost 30 percent of contingents were not included in the survey. Second, the sample represents only a single rotation. Their operational experience may be unique to the circumstances of their mission. Third, the data reflect individual experience, and do not give a clear picture of the collective unit experience. For example, 55 percent of all ranks came under small arms fire at some point in their tour. This gives no indication of frequency: was it a routine or unusual occurrence?

Table 8: Types of Violence

air attack	◆
air threat or demonstration	○
indirect fire	◆
direct fire	◆
ambush	○
sniper fire	◆
active mining	◆
drive-by shooting	◆
attack on installation	◆
projectiles thrown	◆
moves forward in force	○
unauthorized construction	○
restriction of movement	◆
personal threat, intimidation	◆
kidnapping or hostage-taking	◆
riots or civilian violence	○
passive aid to violence	○

◆ = reflected in Eyre survey
○ = not reflected in survey

Despite these shortcomings, the Eyre survey is a useful description of individual operational experience. Eleven of the seventeen types of violence identified in the first chapter are addressed by the survey, some by several questions (Table 8). Together with five questions addressing use of force by peacekeepers, this gives a good picture of individual combat-related operational experience. Seventeen questions address various aspects of contact experience, including meetings and exchanges, social contact, interaction with the media, work with interpreters, negotiations and civil-military cooperation for development.

American Experience in Somalia

A US Army Research Institute (USARI) study describes the results of survey questionnaires from 487 soldiers and interviews with 31 soldiers who participated in Operations Restore Hope and Continue Hope in Somalia.[4]

The focus of the USARI survey and interviews was personnel support and job satisfaction. Many of the questions are therefore of limited relevance to a study of techniques for handling violence.

One set of questions on the events experienced during the Somalia deployment is relevant. This reveals that more than 80 percent of US soldiers surveyed received sniper fire or went on combat patrols and more than 60 percent were targets of indirect fire. Soldiers were not questioned directly about negotiation or other contact skills, but three questions about humanitarian assistance correspond roughly to the Eyre survey's questions about involvement in economic and humanitarian activity. Between a quarter and a third of soldiers in Somalia engaged in humanitarian assistance which must have required some personal contact. A further 65 percent went on what they perceived as "peacekeeping patrols" in which contact with the local population was a significant part of the mission.[5]

Taxonomy of Violent Incidents

The first chapter identified 17 types of violent incidents. These involve the threat or use of force. They are examples only, taken from after-action reports, lessons-learned documents, interviews and accounts of missions. The actions could be directed at UN forces, at the opposing force, or at civilians. Here definitions are offered for the incidents identified in the first chapter.[6]

Five Factors Relevant to Handling Violent Incidents

At least five factors usefully distinguish between types of violence. The first is the ability of parties involved in the incident to communicate directly. In some cases, the "target" can communicate with the perpetrator, but in many cases communication is impossible. This affects the balance of combat and contact skills which are required to handle the incident. The second factor is the degree of belligerent control and anonymity inherent in the incident. This affects the ability of a third party to identify and hold the perpetrator accountable. A third factor is ease of escalation. Some incidents tend to be discreet events, while others are inherently volatile and lend themselves to continuation or escalation unless action is taken. A fourth factor is transience. Some incidents occur and are over, while others leave physical evidence or presence, and the incident continues until this is removed. Finally, some incidents demand a response from high in the command hierarchy, while others can be dealt with at almost any level, depending on the situation. These five factors—communication, accountability, volatility, transience, and response—will influence the ways in which incidents can be managed and de-escalated.

Characteristics of Violent Incidents

In an **air attack** an opposing force aircraft launches bombs or projectiles with hostile intent. In an **air threat or demonstration** it does not actually fire or drop anything, but flies in a hostile or threatening manner. **Indirect fire** involves any fire by a weapon whose crew cannot see the target. Air attack and indirect fire both require some form of command and control if they are to be used effectively. Particularly in the case of air assets, some form of authority is assumed. They can also be tracked precisely if the right resources are available to the peacekeeping force and are well positioned. It should therefore be possible to assign responsibility for these acts and address them through the chain of command responsible for their use.

In practice full accountability for air threat and indirect fire is rarely possible for three reasons. First, the line between civilian and military aircraft and responsibility for control of air-space can be blurred to the advantage of belligerents. In Cyprus, aircraft using the Tymbou airfield routinely violate buffer zone airspace, and are protested whether they are military or civilian.[7] In former Yugoslavia, at least two factions claimed that nocturnal helicopter flights in defiance of the no-flight rules were civilian medical evacuation flights. These are not cases of air attack, but illustrate the general problem of airspace control. Second, UN forces do not normally deploy with target acquisition radar. Even when available, they are insufficient for full coverage. Third, for light mortars and small howitzers, the command and control needed to do random damage is minimal. In conflicts where these weapons are widely available, it is very difficult to determine who is the culprit. The doubts surrounding the mortar blast in a Sarajevo marketplace in 1993 illustrate the problem. Even when a fairly accurate fix on mortar location was provided, doubts remained about who fired it.

The next group of violent incidents could be the result of individual or small group action. Equally, they could be part of an orchestrated campaign directed from any higher level of command. The individuals, groups, weapons used, and even the targets, will not necessarily help to identify the level at which the incident originated. **Direct fire** is fire by a weapon whose crew or firer can see the target. An **ambush** is a surprise attack on a target whose movement is restricted, using direct, indirect and/or physical attack. **Sniper fire** consists of deliberate and accurate single shots from a concealed marksman. It will often be impossible for the peacekeepers under fire to identify *who* is shooting at them, although trained soldiers will know from *where*, and will usually be able to deduce the source. When the report comes to the peacekeepers from one of the parties, the circumstances are even murkier.

Shooting and ambush incidents are life-threatening. The peacekeeper's immediate reaction is to move, take cover, move again while out of sight, then observe and return fire if a target presents itself. These are basic combat skills. The relatively low proportion of UNPROFOR soldiers who fire their personal weapons says as much about the natural advantage of the irregular soldier on his home soil as it does about the restraint of peacekeepers. After the incident, when it is reported by the peacekeepers up their chain of command, it is easy for warring factions to deny knowledge and responsibility or claim provocation. The more unstable the situation, the more plausible are such claims. It is therefore difficult to hold warring factions accountable for their actions against peacekeepers or the other factions.

In urban violence, the stone is everyman's weapon; stones can be lethal. In some cultures, stoning by a crowd is a death-sentence. Most incidents in which projectiles are thrown are not that serious. They are expressions of frustration and discontent. They are more likely to be injurious than fatal. Half the peacekeepers in Croatia and more than three quarters of those in Bosnia reported being the targets of stones or projectiles. It is a common crowd reaction in Somalia and in Lebanon.[8] Rock-throwing mobs, particularly when they include women and children, present special difficulties for the peacekeeper. There is no chain of command, although ringleaders can sometimes be identified. Individuals derive safety from the anonymity of the crowd, and the crowd takes on a dynamic of its own. It may be dangerous or counterproductive for a small number of peacekeepers to attempt to stem the tide of crowd behaviour.[9]

Active mining has occurred in several missions to restrict freedom of movement. Soldiers of a warring faction emplace mines around a target such as a convoy halted on a road, with the intent of blocking further movement. Mining or booby-trapping roads, paths or buildings falls in the same category. Mines may have economic value, too. In Cambodia, minefields force commercial traffic to detour through areas where tribute can be exacted. Knowledge of local minefields is a source of livelihood for guides.[10] In the first case, the culprits are easy to identify. In the other examples, mines are impersonal and cannot be associated with any particular faction. The last examples show that clearing mines may actually run counter to certain interests. Identifying these interests is an important step to handling the proliferation of mines.

Mining presents special difficulties in every category. You cannot negotiate with a mine, and it is frequently unclear who put it there. If one side is mining, the other side is likely to do so, so mining can escalate. The human damage caused by mines, often to non-combatants, can generate increased hostility. Mines are durable, and are expensive and time-consuming to remove. They can be emplaced by the lowest levels in a hierarchy, often without controls, but *stopping* emplacement may take a level of authority no participants have.

Drive-by shootings are rare in most missions. They are characterized by direct fire from a moving vehicle. They are more likely to intimidate than cause fatalities. In Somalia, drive-by shootings and brandishing of weapons from vehicles were used to test the rules of engagement on a routine basis. In most cases it was impossible to tell which faction the vehicle represented. The ease with which narrow streets could be closed off by prearranged crowds meant that the offending vehicles were rarely if ever caught. Once again, there was no accountability for the actions.[11]

In a **physical attack on an installation** soldiers or civilians of the opposing forces forcibly enter or attempt to enter a building or area held against them. These are similar to **moves forward in force**, in which an armed body moves into an area (e.g., a buffer zone) possibly resulting in violent confrontation. These incidents are comparatively rare and represent a major failure on the part of the peacekeeping force. If the attack is launched by one opposing force on the other, the peacekeeping force may be expected to deter the attack by interposing and defending.

When Croatian forces launched an offensive against the Serb-held areas of the Krajina in January 1993, UN forces in one area deployed to defensive positions in a successful effort to deter the attack. The defensive deployment was coupled with intensive negotiating efforts from the UN battalion commander up to the SRSG.[12] Because the attack was obviously directed by legitimate military authorities, the targets for negotiating efforts were clear. Ultimately, defensive deployment and a major negotiating effort were successful and the attack was halted short of incursion into the UN-controlled zone.[13]

In other cases of physical attack, accountability is not so clear. Heavy weapons in the demilitarized zones of the Serbian Krajina were collected and impounded in buildings or militia compounds. During the threatened Croatian attack, a mob attempted to break into one of the compounds to seize weapons for their own defence. It was not immediately clear whether this was an organized attack or a spontaneous outburst, as there were uniformed soldiers, police and civilians in the crowd. In this case, the peacekeepers assigned to guard the compound had to negotiate directly with several ringleaders in an effort to calm the mob and prevent seizure of weapons.[14] When lines have become relatively static, each side may attempt to improve its position. **Unauthorized construction** is the construction of defensive works or installations which may result in confrontation because of their location in an unauthorized area or violation of agreements. It is sometimes possible to identify the level of command which authorized a new construction by the resources which are used. If divisional engineering assets are used to construct an antitank ditch, then the construction was probably authorized at division level or higher. This is an indicator of the appropriate level at which to commence negotiations to remove the violation.

Restriction of movement is one of the most common problems faced by peacekeepers. It entails the use or threat of force to prevent movement on an authorized route. Technically, peacekeepers should have free access throughout the area of operations, so all routes should be open. In practice, each opposing force will attempt to establish limits on the peacekeepers' movements for its own purposes. The origin of the restriction is rarely clear. Is it just the man at the checkpoint who is feeling assertive? Does he have orders to prevent passage? If so, from how high in the chain of command do the orders come? Why were they issued—to prevent the peacekeepers from witnessing something along a route, for general inconvenience, as an assertion of sovereignty? The list of possible reasons will be long.

Restriction of movement creates a real dilemma for the peacekeeper. Often the convoy or patrol will have sufficient force to pass the checkpoint with little risk. But this violates the principle of consent and invites greater threat of violence at the next checkpoint. Local forces will normally have "escalation dominance"— meaning that they can bring more force to bear at a given point than the peacekeeping force under most circumstances. Multiple levels of command also make it possible to claim that the restriction was a misunderstanding; the patrol is prevented from observing an area or event, and the opposing force commander can shrug and say, "Sorry, it won't happen again."

Personal threat or intimidation is threat of violence against a specific individual. It usually occurs in a face-to-face situation, such as a confrontation at a checkpoint or a meeting. The combatant or warring faction normally has superior force available. It can be indirect. One observer reported threats being daubed in blood on the door to UNMO accommodation.[15] It can sometimes be subtle, too. A Canadian officer attended a meeting with one faction in a town where fighting was still going on. The meeting was held on the second storey of a building which was periodically hit by small-arms fire. The officer was seated with his back to a wall of windows, facing counterparts across the room with *their* backs toward the comparative safety of the interior wall.[16] This is a new twist on the old trick of facing one's opponent into the sun!

Personal intimidation may be intended to influence negotiations. It inhibits, but does not always prevent communication. The source of the threat is normally apparent, and is sometimes identifiably unstable. There are accounts of intimidation by swaggering militiamen on checkpoints who are drunk[17] or on drugs[18] and are consequently unpredictable. However intimidation is a transient incident. Where it is used as a deliberate delaying tactic, for example to prevent access to observe an area, it succeeds even while escalation is occurring to counter it.

Kidnapping or hostage-taking is the seizure of an individual, with release made subject to conditions. Like intimidation, kidnapping undermines the security of person on which effective negotiation rests. It can occur in a wide variety of circumstances, from brigandry to a military operation organized at a high level. The Bosnian Serb response to NATO threats of air strikes falls in the latter category.[19] Periodic seizing of UNTAC personnel in Khmer Rouge areas could be classed in the former. Detaining and disarming of UNPROFOR soldiers by local militia forces might fall in the middle.[20] Accountability varies, but can usually be established as being at least as high as the level making the demands associated with seizure. Volatility hinges on risk to the hostages lives, and the incident continues until they are released.

Riots and civilian violence are common elements of protracted social conflict. Unruly or violent demonstrations by civilians may have identifiable objectives, or may be inchoate expressions of frustration and rage. Orderly demonstrations may degenerate if not effectively managed. Demonstrations by one faction may take on enlarged significance if they elicit an official response from another faction.

The "Women's Walk Home" is an annual demonstration in Cyprus in which Greek Cypriot women, some with missing family members or family lands north of the buffer zone, attempt to cross the buffer zone and "walk home" to draw attention to the divided island and occupation by Turkish forces. UNFICYP must preserve the integrity of the buffer zone, and therefore gets involved in crowd control to prevent the demonstration from crossing into the North. In 1989 the demonstration succeeded in occupying a sensitive area inside the walled city of Nicosia, and crossed the buffer zone, resulting in some violence, injuries and arrests. This incident damaged the credibility of UNFICYP and set back relations between the authorities of the North and the Greek Cypriot government.[21]

Although there may be official organizers for a registered demonstration, they may not be in control of events, and cannot necessarily be held accountable for the actions of a mob which gets out of control. Communicating with the many-headed Hydra of an unruly mob is difficult or impossible. Individual behaviour becomes more extreme as people lose their accountability in the anonymity of the mob.[22] A large force may be needed to control a crowd, and the response is likely to be at battalion level or higher. Incidents of mob violence are likely to last for hours, but have been known to endure for much longer.[23]

The last category is **passive aid to violence**. In October 1993 a bitter fight was in progress between Bosnian Muslims and Bosnian Serbs for control of Gorazde— an industrial town South East of Sarajevo. UNPROFOR forces on their way to the town to intervene in the fighting were repeatedly stopped by women and children associated with one faction, deliberately blocking the roads. In this case, the action had the characteristics of a well-organized and comparatively peaceful demonstration, but had a direct impact on the duration of the fighting in Gorazde. In Somalia, controlled crowds were often used to restrict UNOSOM movement, mask the movement of factions, and delay or defeat a response to violence.[24]

Delaying tactics, obstruction and procedural blocks can be used effectively to paralyse UN action against violence. When carried out by crowds, the difficulties noted above probably apply. When checkpoints or military forces are involved, both accountability and communication should be easier.

Implications of Types of Violence for Soldiers

Table 9 summarizes the characteristics of the incident types discussed above. The most important observation is that many of the types of violent incidents typically faced by soldiers at platoon and company level cannot be effectively managed at that level. Well trained and appropriately equipped soldiers can *survive* air attack, indirect fire, sniper fire, mining and intimidation, but they cannot do much about stopping it. Although the table is subjective and impressionistic, it is probably fair to say that only three or four of the incident types can routinely be dealt with through negotiations at the platoon level. Platoon and company level leaders will be involved in the process, but the key to resolution lies higher in the chain of command.

Table 9: Characteristics of Violent Incidents

TYPE OF INCIDENT	1	2	3	4	5
air attack	○	◆	◆	○	○
air threat	○	◆	◆	○	○
indirect fire	○	◆	◆	○	○
direct fire	○	◆	○	○	○
ambush	○	◆	○	○	○
sniper fire	○	○	○	○	○
mining	○	○	◆	◆	○
drive-by shooting	○	○	○	○	○
physical attack	◆	○	○	○	○
projectiles thrown	◆	○	○	○	○
moves forward in force	◆	◆	◆	◆	◆
unauthorized construction	◆	◆	◆	◆	◆
restriction of movement	◆	◆	◆	◆	◆
personal threat	◆	◆	○	○	○
kidnapping, hostage-taking	◆	○	○	◆	○
riots, civilian violence	○	○	○	○	○
passive aid to violence	○	○	○	○	○

1. Can the peacekeeper communicate?
2. Is the perpetrator accountable?
3. Is the incident stable enough to permit negotiation?
4. Does the incident endure long enough to negotiate?
5. Is there a clear party with whom to negotiate?

That platoons and companies, the low end of the military hierarchy, cannot always master their environment is neither surprising nor unique to peacekeeping. A platoon or company commander cannot be expected to influence the launching of air strikes or air threats, nor to prevent mortar shells from falling. This is as true in peacekeeping as in war; in both, the coordination of many different battlefield systems is expected to control the environment within which platoons and companies execute their tasks. Air defence shields soldiers from air attack, target acquisition and counter-battery fire reduce the threat of enemy artillery, intelligence provides advance warning of threats, and so on.

Peacekeeping missions occurring with the consent of the belligerents do not necessarily deploy all the battlefield operating systems required in combat. The gaps in combat capability are filled by contact through the negotiating and liaison system. Here again, Table 9 illustrates the disadvantages faced by individuals and small units dealing with violent incidents. They cannot establish who is responsible for many incidents, nor hold people accountable even if they suspect them. This can only be done effectively by the belligerents themselves. Responding to violence in a way which gets the belligerents to help stop it is the challenge of handling violent incidents.

Handling of Violent Incidents

The surveys of operational experience do not deal directly with the handling of incidents, but can be used to derive conclusions about the balance of combat and contact skills for peacekeepers at various rank levels and in at least the two different sorts of missions represented. The survey's questions can be used to indicate the extent to which peacekeepers experience violence directly, and the extent to which they employ combat skills and contact skills. The conclusion from this survey of experience reinforces the anecdotal observations on the taxonomy of violent incidents; the need for contact skills increases for commanders and staff officers, because those at lower rank levels who experience violence directly are often not in a position to do much about it.

Peacekeepers' Experience of Violence

Eyre's survey includes 22 questions which address experience of violent situations directed at the peacekeeper. The most frequently experienced situations for all ranks in Croatia were contact with mines, being threatened at gun-point, and coming under small arms fire. The top twelve experiences for the buffer zone mission (CANBAT 1 in Croatia) are shown in Figure 11. Each of the remaining ten were experienced by fewer than 10 percent all ranks.

The most common experiences for the convoy escort mission (CANBAT 2 in Bosnia) are shown in Figure 12. Again contact with mines and small arms fire is prominent, surpassed only by exposure to thrown projectiles (usually rocks, according to some comments).

The comparative experience of violence at different rank levels is instructive. The survey identified each respondent by rank. These have been aggregated to reflect three levels: enlisted soldiers, including the junior leadership rank of master-corporal; non-commissioned officers (NCOs), starting at the rank of sergeant; and commissioned officers, from second-lieutenant. In the line companies, sections of ten are commanded by a sergeant, with a master-corporal as his second in command.

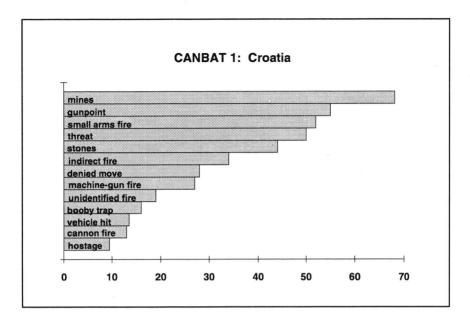

Figure 11: Most Common Experience of Violence Directed at Peacekeepers — Croatia (CANBAT 1)

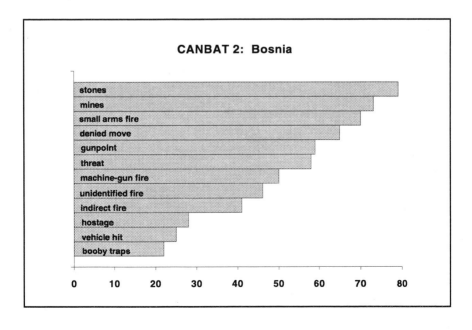

Figure 12: Most Common Experience of Violence Directed at Peacekeepers — Bosnia (CANBAT 2)

The sergeant represents the first rung of supervision, although patrols and convoys will often be commanded by master corporals or even corporals.

The general pattern is that each rank level experiences a bit more violence than its subordinates. Averaging the percentages responding yes to each category yields 21 percent of enlisted soldiers, 25 percent of NCOs and 28 percent of officers. This is reflected in specific categories such as being threatened at gunpoint (57, 59 and 70 percent), being denied freedom of movement (26, 45 and 80 percent) and so on. There are some notable exceptions in both missions: officers are less likely to be stoned, hijacked, disarmed, or held hostage.

The experience of violence is partly a reflection of where peacekeepers are and what they are doing. Some incidents are simply a matter of chance—being in a vehicle which hits a mine or is hit by shell fragments, for example. Others vary with the extent to which a peacekeeper is exposed to routine patrols and regular contact with the belligerents in uncontrolled circumstances.

Any incident which the section handles will normally involve the section commander or his second in command. It will frequently involve the platoon warrant officer (also an NCO) and the platoon commander (a junior officer). When incidents are raised to the company level, they will normally be handled by the company operations officer or the company commander. NCOs in the company command post have an important information handling role, and are sometimes involved in investigations, but will normally remain in the command post, while officers are involved in resolving incidents. This pattern of activity is evident in the combat and contact experiences of enlisted, NCO and officer rank levels.

Experience of Combat

All of the incidents above, in which peacekeepers experience violence directed towards them, are combat experiences. Figures 11 and 12 paint a clear picture of the need for military competence as a prerequisite for presence; lack of familiarity with mines or inability to respond to fire would quickly make a peacekeeping force ineffective in the sort of environment which the Eyre survey reflects.

Five questions in the Eyre survey reflect use of combat skills by peacekeepers which could be classed as "active force." Participants were asked if they fired their personal weapons, fired crew-served weapons, threw smoke or teargas grenades, threw fragmentation grenades; or ordered the use of force in self-defence. The aggregate results are shown for both missions in Figure 13.

The most striking thing about these results is the small proportion of soldiers who used force in comparison to their experience of violence. This was not entirely the result of restrictive rules of engagement. Anecdotally, there were circumstances in which soldiers were explicitly authorized to use force in self-defence, but refrained from firing. This is evident in the survey results. Forty percent of NCOs

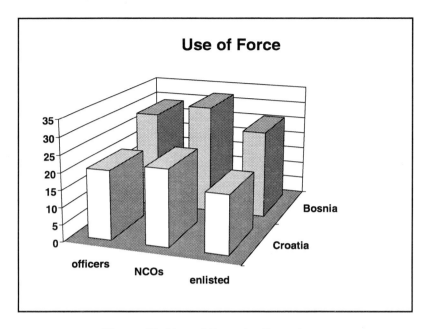

Figure 13: Use of Force by Peacekeepers

gave orders for the use of force in self-defence, and only eight percent of soldiers fired their weapons in self-defence. The orders are precautionary; the shots were fired only when necessary.

The aggregate pattern of use of force is also clear in Figure 13. For both missions, NCOs are the most likely to fire weapons or order the use of force. For CANBAT 2 in Bosnia, the high proportion of mobile convoy duty in which officers were in vehicle cupolas with weapons meant that officers were more likely than soldiers to fire weapons, but still less likely than NCOs. If experiences of violence directed at peacekeepers are included in the figures, the pattern in Figure 13 remains the same.

Experience of Contact

Significantly, the pattern for use of contact skills is different. The Eyre survey includes 17 questions which reflect use of contact skills. Six of these deal with negotiation and mediation in different circumstances, three address social situations, and two each concern meetings, media, economic issues, and language. Across each of these groups and for both missions, the pattern is fairly consistent. Officers experience the most contact, and enlisted soldiers experience the least.

Figure 14 illustrates the strong pattern in experience of contact skills. The pattern has more exceptions in Bosnia than Croatia. For Croatia, only two questions show minor divergence: more soldiers accompanied VIPs, because soldiers were assigned as drivers; and slightly more soldiers than NCOs had social dealings with civilians. In Bosnia, five of the questions diverge, in each case with NCOs showing slightly higher experience levels than officers, for use of language skills, social dealings with military factions, negotiation of freedom of movement, and involvement in

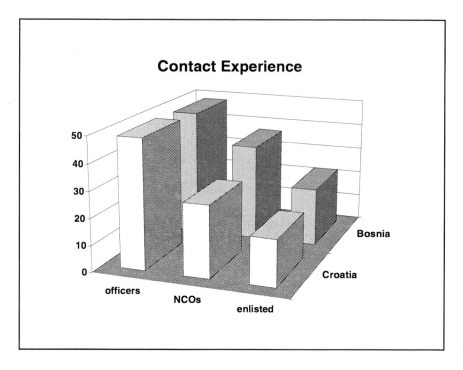

Figure 14: Comparison of Contact Experiences by Rank

economic activity. These are minor differences from a clear pattern which is evident in both missions.

The type of contact experiences also varied by rank. More enlisted soldiers in both missions reported working with interpreters and social interaction than any other contact experience. For NCOs in Croatia, it was the same, but fully three quarters of NCOs in Bosnia experienced negotiating situations. Every officer surveyed in Croatia was interviewed at least once by the Canadian news media, and worked with interpreters making these the most common contact experiences for officers. However, the majority of officers in both missions experienced negotiations with both civilian and military officials.

As with experience of violence and use of force, the experience of contact skills is a reflection of the normal means of handling incidents. For every case were peacekeepers come under fire, or are required to return fire in self-defence, there will be an investigation and a meeting, normally involving interpreters. In the normal process of escalation, the meetings may initially be held at NCO or platoon commander level, and will subsequently involve battalion operations staff and the battalion commander.

Conclusions from the Surveys

Five observations stand out from an examination of the survey responses. First, restraint in the use of force is evident. Overwhelmingly fewer peacekeepers fired their weapons than were fired upon. In Croatia, excluding contact with mines, at least 55 percent came under fire and only three percent, mainly NCOs, fired their personal weapons. In Bosnia, 80 percent had stones thrown at them and fully three quarters came under small arms fire but only four percent fired personal weapons.

Second, contact skills were used by all ranks. A slightly larger percentage of all ranks reported contact than combat experiences. The most common contact experiences were working with interpreters, negotiating with civilian police and belligerent factions, and having social dealings with local civilians.

Third, contact and combat experiences vary by rank, regardless of the type of mission. Both CANBAT 1 in Croatia and CANBAT 2 in Bosnia show increasing exposure to contact experiences with increasing rank. The pattern is the same although the missions are very different.

Fourth, type of contact experiences also varied by rank. More enlisted soldiers in both missions reported working with interpreters and social interaction than any other contact experience. For NCOs in Croatia it was the same, but fully three quarters of NCOs in Bosnia experienced negotiating situations. Every officer surveyed in Croatia was interviewed at least once by the Canadian news media, making this the most common contact experience. However, the majority of officers in both missions also experienced negotiations with both civilian and military officials.

These results suggest that the requirement for contact skills increases with increasing rank; most officers experienced negotiations with opposing forces, while fewer than a third of soldiers did. Part of the explanation for this may lie in the fifth observation. In the majority of violent situations experienced, peacekeepers do not have the opportunity for contact with their assailants. A peacekeeper who comes under direct or indirect fire, encounters a mine, or comes under air attack, for example, does not discuss the issue at the time. It becomes an incident which is dealt with subsequently by his superior NCO or officer.

Self-Defence and Cooperation in Buffer Zones

The conclusions above might lead one to believe that the enlisted peacekeeping soldiers on patrol and in observation posts are almost irrelevant to the handling of violent incidents. They expose themselves to the dangers of mines, small arms fire, artillery and mortar shells, but when incidents occur, they are frequently unable to respond. The response is through commanders and staff officers who meet and negotiate at some distance from the incident. This may affect subsequent incidents, but does not stop the incoming rounds. Are the patrols and observation posts dispensable? Could violent incidents be handled effectively by a network of liaison and observation officers? The UN deploys military observer missions in many cases, and these have an important role to be discussed in a later chapter. However, there is one vital function which unarmed military observers cannot perform. Through their capacity for self-defence, peacekeeping forces contribute to the evolution of tacit cooperation between belligerent forces. How does this work?

There are several processes at the tactical level which assist. The "prisoner's dilemma," military persuasion, and confidence-building are three that are evident from interviews and theory if not from individual surveys.

Prisoner's Dilemma and Buffer Zone Cooperation

Robert Axelrod has described the way in which cooperative systems can evolve by tacit agreement.[26] The "live-and-let-live" system which emerged in the trenches of the First World War illustrates a prisoner's dilemma. There is ample evidence of soldiers deliberately refraining from shooting clearly visible foes. Axelrod explains this by the prisoner's dilemma. Unilateral restraint by the enemy is the most desirable situation, followed by mutual restraint, followed by mutual defection, with unilateral self-restraint being the least desirable situation. The experience of the trenches was that mutual restraint was often achieved. Axelrod demonstrates that the "prisoner's dilemma" of soldiers facing each other across no-man's land induced cooperation as well as conflict, despite the efforts of superior officers to discourage cooperation.

There are direct parallels between the buffer zones established in certain types of peacekeeping missions and the no-man's land of trench warfare. By superimposing a neutral third party, the rewards for mutual restraint are reinforced. This occurs through military persuasion and confidence building. The constant process of patrolling the buffer zone, confronting breaches of the status quo, and escalating protests through both military and diplomatic channels helps to "punish" belligerents for defecting from the cooperative regime. If this works better than the "live-and-let-live" system, it is because soldiers on each side can expect to be punished by their own superiors for defecting.

Effective patrolling and observation is a crucial link in the establishment of a cooperative system. Precise information about who fired what, at what, when, and under what circumstances is vital if the perpetrators are to be held accountable for their actions, reported appropriately, and perhaps even disciplined by their own superiors for breach of instructions. UNFICYP has witnessed Turkish conscripts being beaten with sticks for remaining at a post longer than permitted by local agreements.

Self-defence, "Military Persuasion" and De-escalation

In situations more volatile than Cyprus, the added uncertainty of a response from the peacekeepers acts as a deterrent to violence. The more robust the capacity for self-defence, the more effective the deterrent becomes. Capacity for self-defence is a function of military capability and rules of engagement. A capable force with restrictive rules of engagement has fewer options than one with permissive rules of engagement.[27] Permissive rules of engagement are no help to a force which has little physical capacity for self-defence because of equipment or training deficiencies. Some examples illustrate the ways in which self-defence and the use of combat power at low levels can contribute to de-escalation.

Disarming militiamen and police in the Krajina provides an example. UNPROFOR forces of Sector West were tasked with disarming militiamen and police in the Krajina region in early 1993. Weapons held by individuals included semi-automatic rifles, machine-pistols, and pistols. Antitank weapons and mortars had been moved to caches. Two techniques were used. Suspected caches were cordoned and searched, while individuals with unauthorized weapons were "bush-whacked" and the weapons politely taken.

Cordon and search of suspected caches was conducted as a company-level operation. It was planned in advance based on information from local sources and from battalion operations staff. The operations were coordinated with local authorities and UN Civilian Police, who accompanied the troops executing the search. Light armoured vehicles with heavy machine guns were used to deter interference in the operations, which were sometimes threatened by car-loads of off-duty militiamen. Road blocks, search lights, and the deployment of crew-served weapons on the perimeter led to the impression of overwhelming force, although the mission was usually limited to the seizure of weapons from a single house. In more than a dozen such operations, there were no reports of incidents more serious than scuffles with indignant bystanders, usually dealt with by the civilian police or local authorities.

Individual militiamen and police went about their daily business with personal weapons (automatic rifles and machine pistols) which were unauthorized. Local authorities had agreed to the terms of demilitarization, but were either unable or unwilling to collect weapons from individuals. Rather than confront them at the police stations, individuals on their way to or from work would be surrounded by a section or platoon patrol. The UN section would normally have weapons slung, to avoid the appearance of threat, but they would be wearing fragmentation vests and helmets, and magazines were in the weapons. It was clear to the victim that he was outnumbered. While the victim was detained by the section, a translator would explain the locally agreed regulation about weapons. The explanation was often given at length, to provide an incentive for compliance--if only to get away. The section commander would then provide a receipt for the weapon, and the victim would proceed to work with a chorus of cheerful "good-day" from the section. Several dozen weapons were taken in this manner before unauthorized weapons disappeared from the streets.[28]

Deterring Snipers in Sarajevo. Snipers were a continual problem in Sarajevo, although they varied in competence, motivation, targeting priorities and methods. At least two techniques were used to deal with them.

Where roads were made impassable by periodic or persistent shooting at vehicles, armoured personnel carriers were used as deterrents. They would be parked at critical corners or would patrol the affected streets. Vehicles with machine gun cupolas would traverse to pin-point the direction from which the sniper was firing, and would sometimes respond to shots with short, aimed bursts (usually not effective because of the way in which snipers concealed and protected themselves). According to one account, use of vehicles in this way initially had a deterrent effect, until it became apparent to snipers that they were in little danger.[29]

Where UN armoured vehicles failed to deter, or where lives were threatened, UN "sharp-shooters" would be deployed. Usually from the reconnaissance platoon of infantry battalions, but sometimes just good shots, these soldiers were equipped with improved weapon sights, and used cover and concealment to approach firing positions, and were often successful in killing or driving off snipers. The willingness and ability to defend against snipers by comparable means appears to have been an effective way of reducing their impact.[30] Direct communication in daily meetings with the faction leaders and indirect communication through press conferences which covered shelling and sniping made it clear that military action was purely defensive.

These vignettes suggest important conclusions. The will and capacity for self-defence does contribute to avoiding violence, particularly when the peacekeepers have a temporary advantage, as contrived in each of these cases. However it is essential that any use or threat of force be combined with communication. If this communication cannot be direct (as in the disarming of individual militiamen) it must be indirect, but very explicit (as in the other cases). If this does not occur, then the UN force can expect retaliation the next time it does *not* have an advantage. The purpose of communication is two-fold. It makes the UN intentions clear and reinforces the legitimacy of actions in the eyes of the belligerents.

Rules of Engagement and De-escalation

The rules of engagement in effect in the Krajina and in Sarajevo were comparably restrictive at the time of these incidents. Comparison with the Chapter VII operation in Somalia, UNITAF, suggests some conclusions about the role of uncertainty about rules of engagement in the deterrence of violence.

In the Krajina, UN forces were faced with a potentially explosive situation and quite restrictive rules of engagement. Retaliation, preemption or the prophylactic use of force were not permitted. Only a direct threat to UN personnel or protected persons was justification for use of force. The rules of engagement were classified, and the force went to some lengths to restrict local knowledge of them. Measures included ordering deployments and shows of force by the Sector Reserve,[31] and putting on a firepower demonstration using the TOW-under-armour anti-tank system.[32] The intent of these actions appears to have been to create an impression of strength, resolution and capability. In the case of the TOW demonstration, opposing military commanders were consciously and carefully invited to observe in order to make a point, which was then reinforced through meetings.

In Somalia, the desperate situation facing UN forces and international aid workers in October and November of 1992 led the Security Council to authorize the use of "all necessary means to establish as soon as possible a secure environment for humanitarian relief operations in Somalia."[33] This was, in effect, an enforcement mission. Rules of engagement, however, were based on peacetime employment. Soldiers were directed to use the minimum force necessary under the circumstances, proportionate to the threat.[34] It is difficult to see how they could have been otherwise when most of the contact was with unarmed civilians, and frequently with women and children. Several officers deployed with First Marine Expeditionary Force (I MEF) felt that shows of force in which ringleaders were shot by snipers or armed "technical" vehicles were destroyed by antiarmor vehicles had a salutary effect on reducing incidents of violence.[35] But these shows of force did nothing to deter unarmed civilians, who quickly realized their immunity from retribution. Two effective techniques were avoiding threat situations (using alternate routes or timings, for example) and carrying sticks to repel Somalis with non-lethal force.[36]

The crucial question about rules of engagement and the use of force is the impact it has on the ability of the force to control and de-escalate the number and severity of violent incidents over time. When the source of potential violence is subject to military rationality, permissive rules of engagement can be broadcast as a deterrent. Restrictive rules of engagement should then be kept secret, to avoid tempting opportunistic military forces. In both cases, demonstrated military capability is combined with effective communication to influence the belligerents. On the other hand, when there is no military rationality to the violence (as was often the case in Somalia) then shows of force and deterrence of the sort which were sometimes effective in UNPROFOR are unlikely to be useful. In either case, the less appropriate the rules of engagement are to the situation, the more important it becomes to conceal those rules of engagement. Inappropriate rules of engagement impede a force's ability to deter or control violent incidents, and to defend itself against them.

Confidence Building and De-escalation

Confidence building works at every level from the soldier on the line to military commanders and the national leadership. Confidence in a cease-fire, for example, grows when incidents are handled competently and predictably, precluding benefit to the opposing side. This can be achieved by routine contact and demonstrable impartiality by a competent military force. There is a limit to building trust and confidence at the tactical level, however, because military command structures strive to preserve vigilance and hostility towards opponents. Despite this, there are examples of low-level actions which increase confidence and decrease the likelihood of violent incidents arising.

In Cyprus, the buffer zone is the preserve of UN troops. If one side sees soldiers or civilians of the other side in it, it prompts protests, hostility, and sometimes the risk of escalation even today. In January 1993, a sewer burst in South Nicosia. To repair it, workers from the South had to enter the buffer zone without prior notification. Their presence was noted and protested by soldiers observing from the other side. The sergeant commanding the local UN section invited the soldiers from one side into the buffer zone to assist the workers from the other side. Coffee was sent for. A rare opportunity presented itself, and the sergeant arranged for a group photograph with conscript soldiers, UN soldiers, and grimy sewer workers, arm in arm sipping coffee. Several days later, cheery waves were exchanged between North and South when the workers were back checking on the sewer, again without notification.[37] Repeated incidents like this cannot overcome enforced distrust from the top-down, but they can greatly diminish the risk of accidental escalation of violence.

Belligerents can come to rely too heavily on the UN presence for confidence and security. As a result of force reductions, a number of UNFICYP observation posts ceased to be manned. For years, company commanders in blue berets had met with their counterparts to accuse them of over-manning their observation posts, in defiance of the status quo and local arrangements. In March 1993, a nonplussed commander of City Battery was accused of violating the status quo by *not* manning one of the UN observation posts which had been in place since 1974.

At a slightly higher level, plans to demolish buildings close to the buffer zone in Cyprus were construed by one party as an attempt to create a corridor for an armoured advance. Staff officers were able to provide information about the requirement to destroy some derelict buildings to ensure the safety of people using roads in and near the buffer zone. Careful terrain analysis further convinced both sides that the demolitions did not open up new avenues of approach.[38]

The examples of confidence building at low levels could be multiplied from experiences in UNFICYP, UNPROFOR, and UNIFIL. The prerequisite for confidence building at the lowest levels is direct contact. That contact cannot occur with belligerents unless peacekeepers have the capacity to defend themselves. Weak contingents lacking the confidence for patrols and routine contact with an armed and hostile force do not inspire confidence in the force.

Beyond this basic requirement for self-defence (and self-confidence), the cases at tactical level usually have three elements in common. First, they occur after a rapport has been established between the peacekeeping force and the belligerents. This rapport seems to facilitate communication. Second, they are based to some extent on the expertise or competence of the peacekeepers. In the first example above, it was low-level leadership which converted a confrontation into an opportunity. In the second case it was engineering knowledge and staff expertise, conveyed through a series of complicated meetings at several levels in the chain of command. The third element is that peacekeepers are able to draw attention to the congruent interests of the opposing sides. Like the live-and-let-live system in the trenches, there are times when it is beneficial to cooperate. Every instance in which belligerents are made aware of this is a small boost to their mutual confidence, despite institutionalized vigilance and distrust. When this begins to occur at the tactical level, the mission is ripe for "offensive" action. The combat skills necessary for self-defence are still required, but occasionally take a back seat as even junior leaders use communications skills and leadership to influence their counterparts.

An effective offensive does not originate at the tactical level, but is orchestrated at the operational level, by sector and force headquarters, responding to strategic direction and the aims of the mission. At the strategic level, institutionalized hostility can be undermined by political acceptance of cooperative security arrangements like those embodied in the CSCE process. With political support a new realm of action opens up for peacekeepers: supervision of information exchanges, observation of exercises and training, inter-communal staff talks, and the development of non-military solutions to common defence problems. Contact skills of negotiation, communication, and liaison are paramount. These are areas in which officers in higher headquarters (force level) must develop skills if they are to be useful in the de-escalation and eventual defeat of protracted social conflicts.

Conclusions: Combat and Contact Techniques in the Offense and Defence

In Chapter Two, theories of conflict resolution were used to derive contact techniques to de-escalate protracted social conflicts. The review of evolving military doctrine for peacekeeping in Chapter Three suggests that these contact skills are intimately associated with combat skills. In the early "defensive" stages of de-escalation, peacekeepers use combat and contact skills in tandem to prevent belligerent forces from shooting and moving against each other at the tactical level, which may occur in defiance of consent at the operational level.

This chapter has shown that combat and contact experiences vary by rank. Although both force deployment and communication are required to control violent incidents, soldiers at the lowest levels are inherently limited in their use of contact skills. The surveys of operational experience show that many of the incidents soldiers and NCOs face in a mission like UNPROFOR are not amenable to direct negotiation. This places a premium on both the contact skills of officers and the cohesion of units and headquarters which permits a coordinated response to violent incidents. Despite this limitation, the anecdotes show that formed bodies of troops have an important role in de-escalation, during both the defensive and offensive phases.

The survey data and the anecdotes pose an important question. When violence is successfully controlled at the tactical level, does this have any impact at all at the operational or strategic level? Critics of long-standing and apparently stagnant missions like UNFICYP and UNIFIL would argue that the missions might even be counter-productive.[39] In one sense, the criticism is unfair. Wars are not won by platoon and company actions, nor can peacekeeping missions succeed on the strength of occasional tactical victories. What operational experience of peacekeeping demonstrates is that soldiers win engagements, officers win battles, and commanders and their staffs plan and execute campaigns. This is true of peacekeeping just as it is true in war.

It is to the planning and coordination of campaigns to de-escalate violence that we turn our attention in the next chapter.

Endnotes

1   Charles Dobbie uses the term "management" techniques. See Charles Dobbie, "A Concept for Post-Cold War Peacekeeping," Survival, 36:3 (Autumn 1994).

2   Charles C. Moskos, Jr., Peace Soldiers: The Sociology of a U.N. Military Force (Chicago, IL: University of Chicago Press, 1976); Franklin C. Pinch, "Screening and Selection of Personnel for Peace Operations: A Canadian Perspective," in Peace Operations: Workshop Proceedings edited by David R. Segal, (Alexandria, VA: US Army Research Institute, 1994), 57-80; Johan Galtung and Helge Hveem, "Participants in Peacekeeping Forces," Cooperation and Conflict, 1976.

3   Dr. K.C. Eyre, "General Peacekeeping Survey," Peacekeeping Interview Program (Ottawa, October 1993 - April 1994). Hereafter referred to as the Eyre survey.

4   Joan Harman, "Peacekeeping in Somalia," Research Report 1663, (US Army Research Institute, July 1994), 2-3.

5   Ibid., 11-12.

6   The majority of terms are not defined in standard military lexicons like the Department of Defense Indirect of Military and Associated Terms. The do appear in tactical manuals for units and arms of the service. The definitions offered here are intended to be generic enough to fit the circumstances of peacekeeping rather than be limited to conventional military operations.

7   Interview with an Air Liaison Officer to UNFICYP Headquarters, January 1993.

8   Interviews with Canadian and American participants.

9   Elias Cannetti has described crowd dynamics particularly well in Crowds and Power (Penguin: Harmondsworth, 1973) especially pages 15-87.

10   Interview with a French officer who had commanded troops involved.

11   Interview with an officer of the United States Marine Corps, September 1994.

12   After action report of the 3rd Battalion Princess Patricia's Canadian Light Infantry, as discussed by a former commanding officer, and various internal UNPF documents.

13   Unclassified extracts from after action reports and open news sources.

14   Interview with a Canadian company commander, May 1993.

15   Interview with a Canadian serving as a UN Military Observer, March 1994. The incident occurred in UNPROFOR, Sector South, in 1993.

16   Interview with a Canadian staff officer in Headquarters, Sector West, UNPROFOR.

17   Interview with a former company commander, May 1993.

18   Such as Khat, Center for Army Lessons Learned, Somalia Special Edition No. 93-1, (January 1993), 30.

19   Interview with a Canadian staff officer in Sector South, UNPROFOR, October 1994.

20   Unclassified extracts of after action reports, OP CAVALIER, 19 April 1994.

21   UNFICYP documents. Interview with a Canadian officer who participated, January 1993.

22   Canetti, op. cit.

23   The Intifada is an example of protracted and organized civil violence which is impervious to communication, exhibits minimal accountability, and can be highly volatile.

24   CALL after-action reports.

25   The general pattern shows up for both CANBAT 1 in Croatia and CANBAT 2 in Bosnia when averages are used, and becomes more marked if only the most frequently experienced incident types are used. There are some exceptions in Bosnia. A smaller proportion of

officers than NCOs experienced being verbally threatened (57, 76 and 67 percent), being denied freedom of movement (63, 83, 82 percent), and coming under small arms fire (74, 83 and 67 percent) for example.

26 Robert Axelrod, The Evolution of Cooperation (New York, Basic Books, 1984).

27 These relate to the concept of broad and narrow interpretations of self defence discussed in Chapter Three.

28 Interview with a Canadian company commander, May 1993.

29 Interview with a Canadian liaison officer serving with the battalion involved, May 1993.

30 Interview, Major-General Lewis MacKenzie, February 1995.

31 Interview with a Canadian staff officer in October 1993 at St. Hubert, Quebec, concerning events in UNPROFOR in May 1993.

32 Interview with a Canadian staff officer on 19 October 1994 at Leavenworth, Kansas, concerning events in UNPROFOR, May-June 1994.

33 Security Council Resolution 794 (1992) cited in United Nations Peacekeeping Update: May 1994 (New York: Department of Public Information, 1994), 103.

34 Jonathan T. Dworken, "Rules of Engagement: Lessons from Restore Hope," Military Review (September 1994), 27-28.

35 Interview with an American officer in September 1994 at Fort Leavenworth, Kansas concerning events in December 1992 - January 1993, which he observed while serving with I MEF.

36 JTF Somalia, Staff Judge Advocate, Operation Restore Hope After Action Report/Lessons Learned (March 1992), 21.

37 Interview with officers and NCOs of City Battery, 1st Regiment Royal Canadian Horse Artillery.

38 D.M. Last, "Peacekeeping Doctrine and Conflict Resolution Techniques," Armed Forces and Society, 22:2 (Winter 1995/1996). This and related cases are described in UNFICYP and Canadian contingent files.

39 Paul F. Diehl, "When Peacekeeping Does Not Lead to Peace: Some Notes on Conflict Resolution," Bulletin of Peace Proposals 18:1 (1987), 47-53.

Chapter Five

Orchestrating De-Escalation Campaigns

The essence of de-escalation is reducing the number and severity of violent incidents over time. De-escalation campaigns aim to do this by tying the resolution of individual incidents into a larger pattern of compliance with agreements into which the belligerents have entered. More ambitious campaigns go further to undermine the causes of violent behaviour, pushing de-escalation toward eventual resolution. Conflict resolution theory presented in Chapter Two demonstrates the importance of de-escalation as part of a continuing process. The control and de-escalation of incidents is only the initial "defensive" action.

Chapter Three on doctrine and practice underscored the importance of consent at the operational level if active force is to be used at the tactical level for other than self-defence. In the emerging doctrine of wider peacekeeping, consent facilitates the use of force when it is necessary, and contact at every level helps to build the consensus which avoids the need for force. The surveys of operational experience outlined in Chapter Four, however, demonstrated that many of the violent situations faced by soldiers do not permit them to use contact skills directly. Faced with bombs and bullets, they react with basic combat skills, and indirect negotiations are conducted by higher authorities—often after the incident is over. Campaigns to control and de-escalate violence must therefore be orchestrated at least at the battalion level, and usually at sector or force level. In other words, the de-escalation of violence is the operational art of peacekeeping.

This chapter addresses two questions relevant to campaign planning for de-escalation. How are contact and combat skills orchestrated to achieve de-escalation? And what opportunities are there for "offensive" action against the roots of the conflict, by military forces? The cases presented in this chapter are not definitive descriptions of any of the events discussed. They are selected only to illustrate processes for combining combat and contact techniques in campaigns of de-escalation at the tactical and operational levels.

De-escalating Incidents and De-escalation Campaigns

Incidents exhibit a certain dynamic over time. The escalation and de-escalation of individual incidents is sometimes a microcosm of the relations between opposing forces and the UN. UNFICYP provides some examples. Time and space are compressed and the scene has been repeated sufficiently in Nicosia for the pattern to be clear. General Lewis MacKenzie described a scene from 1965 which might equally have occurred any time up to 1989:[1]

> The disturbance was usually nothing more than bored solders having a bit of fun.
>
> The favourite verbal gambit was to accuse the enemy conscript opposite your position of arriving on this earth as a result of frequent out-of-wedlock activities by his mother or, better still, as the result of a liaison between his mother and a farm animal. This frequently drew a response that North Americans would refer to as "mooning" . . . frequently the "exposee" would attempt to strike the exposed part. . . with a well-aimed rock. . . .[2]

Bored young men shout, throw stones, and in some cases it escalates to shots. Commanders, disingenuously or not, often read deliberate provocation into these incidents. In 1984 and again in 1988 shooting deaths on the line which were probably accidental resulted in a public furore in the Greek-Cypriot press which obscured all rational dialogue at a political level for a period of several months. The deaths were cited in the media campaign to prevent General Greindl's proposed demilitarization of old Nicosia, where most of these incidents occurred.[3]

The importance of these incidents in perpetuating the cycle of violence and hatred cannot be over-emphasized. Elias Canetti has described how every death can become a symbol for mobilizing vengeful crowds.[4] Kaplan writes about a 26-year-old Albanian describing atrocities from the Second World War: " . . . he had no personal knowledge of the events he described. Rats infest his house, he told me. The Serbs were to blame."[5] Individual incidents, initially real and eventually the imagined and folkloric images of those incidents, become the fuel for continuing violence from the lowest level, regardless of any progress towards a strategic settlement. The task of the peacekeeper is not merely to control incidents, but to begin the long process of burying hatreds which are carefully nurtured from generation to generation. This second part of the job is the offensive element in campaigns to control and prevent violence.

As discussed in Chapter Four, de-escalation can be supported by physical presence and use of the chain of command to impose control and accountability. Physical presence can prevent immediate escalation. Meetings at platoon, company and battalion level can minimize the recurrence of incidents over time. Unit records from a stable peacekeeping operation like UNFICYP show how frequently meetings are held at company level (usually at least weekly). There is a correlation between the number of incidents and the number of meetings held, although it tends not to be a particularly strong one in the UNFICYP case.[6]

Interviews and personal observations reveal common patterns in the sequence of negotiations to control incidents, and common lines of argument used by UN negotiators at platoon and company level.[7] One of the warring factions will commit a violation. Commonly it will claim provocation or self-defence. The UN negotiator may present facts indicating that both sides have engaged in provocative acts, or that the number and severity of incidents is intolerable. The UN officer may appeal to professionalism: "you can control your subordinates' actions, can you not?" "Soldiers will be soldiers, but in the interests of common safety, you must control your soldier's actions; put yourself in the opposing commander's shoes; what would you do if. . . . " and so on.

The effectiveness of these relatively standard lines of negotiation at low level will depend partly on whether the incidents being protested are linked or isolated. Even in the comparatively simple environments of UNFICYP and UNIFIL, the opposing forces will sometimes launch a series of incidents for a particular purpose.[8] One of the first steps in devising a campaign plan to de-escalate a series of incidents is to determine whether they are linked or isolated.

Linked Versus Isolated Incidents

In a radio documentary entitled "Sniper," the Canadian Broadcasting Corporation interviewed a woman from Sarajevo, formerly a markswoman in European and Olympic competitions, who was waging a private war amidst Sarajevo's disintegrating order. Her actions were independent and uncontrolled, influenced by her daily efforts to survive and the targets presented by opportunity.[9] Not all sniping in Sarajevo is as random as this case, however. Both sides used sniping fire in apparently conscious attempts to control life in Sarajevo, particularly the use of main roads and movement between communal enclaves. Food lines, convoy routes and approaches to the airport were targeted to restrict movement.

At meetings between the UN and warring factions the subject of sniping was raised repeatedly, and control or reduction of sniping incidents was occasionally tied explicitly to demands by one side or the other.[10] This deliberate manipulation of level of sniping implies instructions from commanders to soldiers, although the degree of control may have been less than perfect.

Indirect fire is normally more controlled than direct fire, because of the manpower needed to move quantities of ammunition, the cost of the rounds, and the command and control necessary to engage targets effectively. Yet there are examples of isolated incidents of indirect fire, too. By mid-1994, heavy weapons within 20 kilometers of Sarajevo were collected in "weapons collection points" which really amounted to supervised firing positions. A UN observer would monitor these weapons, frequently by sitting around the brazier with their crews. This was the situation when a disgruntled militia-man stalked across the position and dropped two shells in a mortar tube before anyone could stop him, then sat down. There was a flurry of activity, and the commander came to explain to the UN observer that the man's daughter had been killed that morning, and he was taking vengeance. The observer called his counterpart on the opposite hill and told him that the rounds had been a random act and would not be repeated if there was no retaliation. In this case, the incident did not escalate to an exchange of fire.[11] It is easy to see how isolated acts of individual vengeance can be construed as deliberate breaches of a cease-fire, permitting escalating violence. But it can also be seen that isolated violent acts are easier to offset than planned and sequenced acts of violence. Other reports from the same area indicated consistent provocation by one warring faction or the other, with the intent of stimulating an over-reaction which might be used for propaganda purposes.[12]

The phenomenon can also be illustrated with restrictions to movement. Sometimes there appears to be no rhyme or reason to the intransigence of low-ranking officers or soldiers manning road-blocks. Bureaucratic procedures are used to delay and block convoys one day, and not the next. These incidents are so idiosyncratic as to defy categorization; it is frequently difficult to determine who is in charge at checkpoints, let alone why the delay is imposed.[13] On the other hand, some delays are clearly linked to superior commanders' operational objectives. During the Medak pocket operation the UNPROFOR advance was held up for 12 hours (according to a negotiated time line) with mines and road-blocks, while one faction destroyed villages.[14]

The Need For a Coordinated Response—Escalation

The initial action to deal with these incidents is the same whether they are isolated or linked by some ulterior design of the warring factions. Investigations and low-level negotiations are used to explore the situation and attempt resolution. If progress is made at low levels, this may be a sign that the incidents are isolated. It is often difficult to tell whether progress is being made or not. After a transient event like a stray shooting, a "good" meeting might extract an apology—"sorry, it won't happen again."—while a "bad" meeting might yield nothing more than denial, bluster, and accusations. Neither outcome seems to relate to whether the incident will be repeated or not. Patterns of events emerging within a particular opposing force commander's area of operations can indicate a larger problem, and can be raised as a negotiating point. "We see far more violations in your area than in the adjacent area over the last three weeks. . . ." This opening might be linked to a consultative approach, if there is a good working relationship between the UN and opposing force commanders.[15] Consultation might offer alternatives for ammunition controls, improved supervision, notification of local training, and so on.

The other side of the coin is that incidents may be directed by higher authorities. Commanders may expect a certain amount of hostile activity from their subordinates, regardless of local tranquillity. In the First World War, superior officers and new-comers periodically tried to shake the live-and-let-live cooperation which evolved between opposing forces in the trenches.[16] Artillery schedules were a popular means for doing this, because artillery was less vulnerable to retaliation than were the front-line trenches. Its firing could also be verified.[17] Combatants in Bosnia may have found a way around this problem. Mortar and artillery duels consisting of hundreds or thousands of rounds were fired, apparently in response to direction. There are sometimes no casualties because each side appears to have warned the other of the time and intended targets; shells fall on bare hills or empty trenches. UN protests to higher commanders help the subterfuge, because commanders have confirmation that their orders are carried out, though they may be unaware of the tacit collaboration to avoid casualties at a lower level.[18]

Both the directed artillery barrages and their evolution towards a live-and-let-live system illustrate the need for a coordinated response at multiple levels to stifle cease-fire violations and to take advantage of the dynamics of cooperation.

Illustrating Escalated Negotiations

The coordination of escalated negotiations can be illustrated with a typical civil-military incident. A pair of tracked vehicles had crossed a seeded field to observe from a hill. While trying to cross back to the road, a civilian car pulled in front and another pulled up behind, hemming the vehicles in. An angry crowd gathered, including women and children, and men brandishing weapons. Some tried to climb on the vehicles. The platoon commander and company commander were both on leave, and the platoon warrant officer was with the vehicles, while the company second-in-command was at the command post. The platoon warrant officer asked permission to open fire to dispel the crowd. Permission was denied; the presence of women and children in the crowd indicated that there was not an immediate threat to life. Because two key officers in the chain of command were absent, there was a risk of escalating immediately to the battalion commander for a minor incident, setting a bad precedent.

In these circumstances, a neighbouring company commander or other field officer substituted to provide another link in the chain of escalation. The warrant officer could not negotiate with credibility; as the commander on the scene who was engaged in the incident, his objectivity was compromised. Like a squad leader pinned down by fire, his role was to "fix the opposition" and call for support from higher. "Fixing the opposition" consisted of three steps. First, identify the parties with whom negotiations must be conducted, in this case they were the farmer whose fields had been damaged and the village mayor. The latter was important for subsequent dealings. Second, separate the negotiating party from the crowd by taking the two men to one side. Third, set up the meeting time and place. This implies identifying a secluded place appropriate for conducting a meeting, in this case a barn, and arranging for a place to contact the arriving superior.

When the neighbouring company commander arrived, he was met at the edge of the field with salutes and a show of respect from the soldiers in place. This showed the crowd that an important person had arrived, and conferred importance on the people chosen to speak with him. He then removed his flak vest and weapon, gave them to his driver, and greeted the farmer and mayor courteously. They met at the barn, the UN providing coffee and cigarettes. The incident was defused with offers of compensation. This opened channels between the mayor and the G5 (civil military affairs) for routine communications about damage caused by the UN, and subsequent incidents were avoided. Explaining the claims process to local farmers and preventing abuses became part of the G5 responsibilities at sector level.[19]

This incident illustrates three points about de-escalation of incidents and the launching of local campaigns. First, the commander involved in an incident becomes part of the problem; he must set the scene for others to resolve it, usually at the next level up in the chain of command. Second, identifying the right people to talk to is crucial both to resolving the incident and to expanding the solution to prevent future incidents. Usually this involves implicating someone in higher authority, even when there is no "chain of command." In this case, getting the village head or mayor involved in the claims process was a key step. Third, identifying and addressing the source of the incident and *finding the right level to address it* lies at the heart of preventing future incidents. It is seldom as straightforward as this example.

These three points form the interface between dealing with incidents at the tactical level and orchestrating campaigns to reduce the frequency and severity of incidents at the battalion, sector and force level.

One of characteristics of escalation is that it can occur along several quite different lines. For example, it might occur through parallel military structures, within any number of civilian hierarchies, or laterally amongst civilian authorities and non-governmental agencies.[20] Some of these alternatives will be illustrated in the cases which follow.

Factors In Orchestrating Campaigns

The theory, doctrine and experience reviewed in earlier chapters yields important factors for planning and orchestrating a campaign of de-escalation.

What Theory Tells Us

Theory of conflict resolution reviewed in Chapter Two suggested the importance of achieving physical separation as a prerequisite to controlling physical violence. A political officer writing on the shortcomings of UNPROFOR has testified to the wisdom of that lesson. "In Bosnia, any implementation plan must provide for the separation of forces in an effective way. The preferred alternative to separation along a confrontation line is separation of belligerent forces through buffer zones."[21] The real contribution of theory is in pushing de-escalation beyond defensive measures to attack the roots and causes of conflict.

Theory suggests that de-escalation campaigns should make provision for changing attitudes and beliefs over time. The third party must make conscious efforts to cater to the identity and security needs of all parties to the conflict. This entails identifying structural violence, abusive patterns of ownership or exploitation of labour, education inequalities, and differences in quality of life and expectations over time. Clearly these are long term issues which are beyond the scope of a military force. In the short term, however, the military force may be engaged in efforts to bring parties together across communal lines. Public information programmes and psychological operations may play a part in this.

What Doctrine Tells Us

Doctrine focuses mainly on combat skills, as noted in Chapter Three. Individual combat skills are vital for force protection. Collective combat skills are essential to conduct operations, interposing and posturing with forces to deter aggression, control areas, support negotiations to reduce violence, and so on. Doctrine also suggests that individual soldiers should have basic contact skills for handling crises or difficult situations like hostage-taking or checkpoints, and that key staff officers should have advanced contact skills for managing meetings, three party mediation efforts, the use of translators and interpreters and so on.

However, military peacekeeping doctrine does not provide any guidance on the use of conciliation, arbitration, good offices, nor on the techniques for using force deployment to enhance bargaining positions. Although several checklists for investigations and negotiations are provided, there is little discussion of prescriptive negotiating technique, and the elicitive conflict transformation techniques which have been explored by civilians are not found anywhere in military literature. Military doctrine deals effectively with the *defensive* handling of incidents, but not with the development of *offensive* campaigns.

What Experience Tells Us

Evidence from interviews, after-action reports and surveys suggests that the will and capacity for self-defence helps deter violence directed against peacekeepers. Communications, frequent if not continuous contact and negotiations with the warring factions are essential elements of the system which prevents escalation of violence, and frequently prevents the need for use of force in self-defence. Anecdotes from stable situations also suggest that confidence-building can work from the lowest levels, given appropriate opportunities for contact and the tacit permission of superiors.

Assessing Campaigns

Given this basis of experience, theory and doctrine, how are we to assess examples of de-escalation campaigns? We need means of comparing the circumstances in which combat and contact skills have been combined to achieve de-escalation. The criteria are taken from the theory of conflict resolution and third party intervention reviewed in Chapter One.

Context of the Conflict

In Chapter Two, the causes of escalation were presented, along with two models for de-escalation (Mitchell's dynamic protraction model, and Ron Fisher's contingency model). The factors identified there constitute key elements in the context of a conflict or series of incidents which staffs are attempting to control. A joke told in Bosnia begins with a peasant finding a magic frog who offers him one wish, but warns him that whatever he gets, his neighbour will get double. The peasant thinks for a while, then wishes, "Make me blind in one eye!" This illustrates an aspect of the dynamics of escalation which Wall has identified: a history of antagonism; festering resentment; parties not concerned with costs, and so on. Preventing escalation and working toward the indicators of de-escalation (mutual conciliatory gestures, voluntary yielding, change of goals) is an important part of campaign planning.

The Mitchell and Fisher models present a more complete picture of the potential de-escalation process. Military peacekeepers are generally occupied with the early defensive stages: segregation, stopping the violence. It is in these early stages that combining combat and contact skills is particularly crucial. By the time that a conflict has de-escalated to routine pre-negotiation contacts and problem-solving dialogues, or even to the stage of stagnant stand-off now existing in Cyprus, the risks of miscalculating force deployment are greatly reduced. On the other hand, peacekeepers acting as go-betweens may increase the risk that parties will avoid direct contact, and the conflict will be perpetuated. The cases below highlight the problems inherent in the early stages of de-escalation.

Nature of the Conflict

In Chapter Four, the characteristics of various types of violent incidents were assessed; some lend themselves more readily to accountability and direct negotiations than others. About half of the types of violence experienced by peacekeepers can be defended against, but are not susceptible to direct negotiation (Table 7, Chapter Three). Others which involve physical attack may permit direct negotiation, but must be supported by measures to defend the force under threat. Of the cases examined below, the majority required defensive action and indirect negotiation.

The type of violent incident and the ways in which the violence is linked to other issues are important factors in devising a campaign plan. There are parts of the confrontation line in Croatia and in Bosnia where people and goods associated with the black market passed freely across, and where belligerents halted hostilities at scheduled intervals to trade. Bandits from both sides who profited from the shortages in Sarajevo were believed to have been behind much of the shooting at humanitarian aid flights.[22]

Violence for profit, however, is probably the exception. Conflict research suggests that excitement and fear in crises, hatred built upon generations of learned enmity, and the logic of realpolitik are the most common correlates of violence in protracted social conflict.[23] Violence stemming from fear and excitement is a short-term phenomenon with long-term implications, as discussed above. It can be dampened by physical separation, and by guarantees of security on either side of the separation. Hatred of the sort described above can only be changed gradually; this is a task transcending generations. Finally the logic of realpolitik can be overcome by concrete demonstrations of common interest and the benefits of cooperation, under some form of third party supervision which overcomes mutual distrust. The UNHCR's bicommunal work in Cyprus, which requires participation by both Greek- and Turk-Cypriots to gain access to a lucrative pot of project funds is an example of this last.[24]

Characteristics of Parties Involved

It is apparent from the discussion above and in previous chapters that the cohesion and responsiveness of the chain of command is perhaps the most important factor in dealing with parties to the conflict. Returning to Wall's framework for analysis of third party intervention (Figure 2 in Chapter One) the relationship between the points of contact and their constituents is important in determining the relative effects of force deployment and direct contact. It also influences the scope for indirect communication (for example, through the media) which might be used to affect the situation.

Information about the coherence of opposing forces may be incomplete. In UNFICYP it can be assumed that both parties are well controlled, and ill-discipline is the cause of only rare and minor incidents. In UNIFIL, at least one party denies control over armed factions which may be used to achieve military objectives.[25] In UNPROFOR, peacekeepers are rarely certain of the degree of control exercised by their counterparts or their counterparts' superiors. This lends great importance to force protection, multiple levels of liaison, verification of information, and avoiding reliance on guarantees which may be worthless.

Intervention Strategy

Intervention strategy is the manner in which combat and contact skills are used by the military force. It includes the deployment of other assets to influence the situation. UNMOs, ECMs, directed aid and civilian assistance are all of interest. For my purposes, the combination of force deployment and negotiation is the main focus.

Both combat and contact techniques form part of the communication between UN "mediators" and the parties to the conflict. The framework depicted in Figure 2, Chapter One, can be expanded to show the uncertainty with which these means of communication are actually used. Ron Fisher refers to encoding and decoding messages, since even the clearest signal or message must pass through layers of interpretation and reaction. This is illustrated in Figure 15.

What Figure 15 illustrates is the imprecision of communication in a peacekeeping setting. When an aid convoy is shelled (a public, observable action)

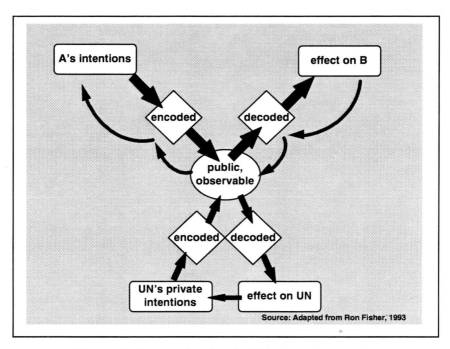

Figure 15: Communicating the Third Party's Intentions

that is a form of communication. What does it mean? The convoy was on its way to a Muslim enclave. Were the Serbs shelling it (to stop it from getting there)? Were the Muslims shelling it (to incriminate the Serbs)? Was a bandit group shelling it (to pick up the pieces)? Even the "observable event" is often suspect. How many people died in a particular mortar attack? If the party originating the incident cannot be ascertained, how can the encoded intents be accurately divined?

So far I have addressed only the horizontal chain between A and B in Figure 15. UN intervention strategies are complicated by the multiplicity of "private intentions" within the organization, and frequently by diffusion of effort. This is not altogether a bad thing. Game theory experiments indicate that cooperation can emerge when players are uncertain about the reactions of opponents.[26] Nevertheless, there are also good examples of cooperative restraint achieved by unequivocal communication: "We never use our [rifle grenades] unless the Germans get particularly noisy, as on their system of retaliation three for every one of ours come back."[27]

All this means three things for assessments of intervention strategy. First, what is the third party reacting to, or trying to achieve? Second, does clarity or obfuscation of communications serve the interests of peace better? Third, what is the best balance of combat and contact to convey the message, and will it be appropriately (not necessarily equally) understood by all parties?

An example from the UN deployment in Croatia illustrates the problem at the operational level. Reacting to fighting between the Jugoslav National Army (JNA) and Croatian Guard, the Vance Plan of November/December 1991 provided for separation along a cease-fire line, mutual withdrawal of JNA and Croatian Guard units, and other provisions relating to UN Protected Areas (UNPAs). The overall status of the UNPAs was never settled as part of the Vance plan. The observable fact was that a "protection force" was occupying an area inside the borders of Croatia; Croatian officials "decoded" this as protection of Croatian sovereignty; the Krajina Serbs "decoded" it as protection for the nascent Republic of Serbian Krajina.[28] The uncertainty helped maintain a stand-off for a while, but resulted in two attacks mounted on the "pink zones" in January and September 1993. The clear communication of well-dug-in defensive positions and carefully sited machine guns had to compensate for the lack of clarity in the Vance plan. In Sector West, along the Zagreb-Belgrade highway, the military communication was unequivocal, and the Croatian advance stopped. In four other areas (including the Maslenica Bridge, and Zemunic airfield) the communication was not as clear, nor the defences as robust. In these areas, tensions continued for some time.

These four factors--context, conflict, parties and intervention strategy--will be assessed for each of the examples of campaigns.

Campaigns to Stop Direct and Indirect Fire

The small arms and artillery fire around Sarajevo attracted a lot of international attention. Its persistence demonstrated UNPROFOR's inability to keep the peace, and it became part of the intricate psychological warfare being waged in the international media by all the parties to the conflict, including the UN. Could it be stopped? Below are two accounts of recent campaigns to quell the shooting in various parts of Bosnia.

Stopping the Sniping

The importance of a robust response for deterrence was mentioned in Chapter Four. The dynamics, however, may be complex and variable. Interviews with battalion-level officers suggested that sniping declined when Warrior armoured fighting vehicles began to traverse their turrets to cover snipers while they moved down various notorious "snipers' alleys."[29] Officers at sector Headquarters, however, had a different view of events. One suggested that the number of sniping incidents actually increased when the traversing policy came in. Snipers knew that a moving Warrior vehicle could not hit them, and treated the threat as a challenge.

Action taken at sector level was two-pronged. First, an effort was made to identify all firing positions on both sides. The positions were mapped, and each side was presented with a map of its own positions. Meetings stressed the adverse effects of the firing, and requested the commanders to take action to ensure that "unauthorized firing" did not take place in their areas. Simultaneously, battalions were asked to stop the policy of pointing at sniping positions. According to officers at sector level, this two-pronged strategy worked to reduce the number of sniping incidents.[30]

It is probable that some of the sniper fire was officially directed, with the balance being "freelance." Robust self-defence and contact was aimed at the official sniping, and the maps helped to make the unofficial snipers part of the belligerents' responsibilities. It should be noted that headquarters staff officers associated with "military information" (or intelligence) were generally less sanguine about the effectiveness of tactics deemed effective at battalion level, but did not have alternatives to offer.

Stopping Indirect Fire on Convoys

Reporters sometimes describe indirect fire and sniping as "anonymous." Sniper fire can be, but indirect fire need not be. Even in the absence of mortar-locating radar, the science of crater analysis can often pinpoint the origin of fire with almost forensic precision. To do so requires training, expertise, firing data for the weapons in use, and timely analysis. Putting these assets together was part of a civil-military relations campaign to reduce indirect fire harassment of humanitarian activity in Bosnia.

In May 1993, mortar and artillery attacks in Sarajevo had brought the city to a standstill. The attacks were not random. Shelling reports allowed operations staffs to build up a picture of where and when attacks were occurring. Bread lines at queuing time, cemeteries during funerals, even schools as children came out were targets. There was systematic targeting of civilians, in clear violation of international conventions and law of war. Initially, the assumption was made that if one side was being hit, another faction must be responsible. This assumption sometimes proved to be ill-founded.

The first response was to send shell reports alone to both sides. Each blamed the other. A Ukrainian battalion deployed with mortar-locating radar, and was put out of action within days. UN staff officers assumed that part of the problem was that Muslim and Croat factions had targeted it because of the "confessional affiliation" between Ukrainians and Serbs, casting aspersions on any of the data produced by the battalion. It was at this stage that the staff resorted to crater analysis.

The soft concrete and tarmac roads yield very accurate patterns which often permit sources of the fire to be located with great accuracy. Mortar fins, shell fuses and fragments can be used to identify the type of weapon. After one attack, the date, time, and location of the attack, the fuse and lot number of the shells, and the location of the battery was provided to the offending faction. This kind of precision was sufficient to launch charges of violations of the laws of war, which may have been implied in some meetings. Humanitarian aid workers and military observers were taught to use crater analysis, and the frequency and accuracy with which the offenders were identified increased dramatically. At least one road closed by shelling was reopened when the faction which had denied responsibility was presented with proof, threatened with publicity, and stopped shelling.[31]

The belligerents did not accept this attempt to make them accountable for indirect fire. In addition to repeated attempts to take radar out of action, UN personnel attempting to analyze craters became targets of choice for snipers. A drill was developed in which a convoy of armoured vehicles would form a ring around the point of impact, protecting it while the analysis was conducted.[32] The factions moved firing positions as close as possible to the confrontation line, to make the task of identifying the point of origin more difficult. When mortar fire killed an observer, investigators arrived on the scene within hours to find that the craters had already been deliberately obscured.[33]

There are two endings to this story. From the point of view of the civil-military relations staff officer and the humanitarian aid convoys, a temporary lull in artillery and mortar attacks was achieved and the campaign was a success. When consistently and vigorously applied and linked to meetings and press conferences, crater analysis helped to make factions accountable for their actions. From the point of view of the military intelligence officer, little long-term change in the pattern of shelling was noted; some months were better, some were worse.

Assessment of Campaign Factors

Factors permitting the escalation of the sniping and shelling battle in Sarajevo can easily be identified from Wall's list. One faction clearly perceived that it had a power advantage, and was determined to use it. There were no effective limits on actions, and the Muslims in particular were trapped and could not escape the conflict. Both sides show a complete failure to identify with the other side. Part of the explanation for this may lie in the conflicting identities of cosmopolitan city dwellers besieged by country dwellers who did not value the culture of the city.

The shelling and sniping around cities should not be interpreted strictly in terms of military value. Hatred is probably the most common element in the destruction of cities and their inhabitants in protracted social conflicts. Bosnia and Croatia are not unique in this respect, though it is there that the phenomenon has been most frequently described recently:

> A typology of hatred could be developed. For example, a type of hatred is that against anything bearing the signs of a different culture. Another type is hatred against urban life, its tolerance and its cosmopolitan spirit. There is hatred for and destruction of cities, though they may not even have been military objectives with any strategic importance. Vukovar, Durbrovnik, Sarajevo. . . . pearls of culture and civilization. These were not vital military objectives destroyed to defeat the adversary. Their destruction was meant to dishearten the civilians and annihilate coexistence.[34]

It is probably a combination of the hatred, lack of identity and power advantage of those on the outside (abetted by provocation for strategic purposes from the inside) which perpetuated the shelling and sniping in the Sarajevo area.

The degree of control over belligerents by their commanders was incomplete in both the shelling and sniping cases. Although heavy weapons had been collected, the control over the collection points was imperfect because of the mountainous wooded terrain, numerous firing points, limited number of observers, and restrictions on freedom of movement. Many smaller mortars remained at large, particularly within the city, and were frequently used to provoke retaliation for propaganda purposes. Whether such uses were officially condoned is almost a mute point; it is questionable whether either warring faction could control all its assets, even with UN assistance.

The strategy in both cases involved two dimensions. First, the sources of the sniping and indirect fire were physically identified, confirmed and proof was collected. This was largely a military function, involving patrols, observation, crater analysis, artillery location technology, mapping and triangulation. Information about the effects of the fire on civilians was equally important. Connecting a large number of shell reports and battery identifications with firing at civilian targets made a particularly damning indictment for presentation to the respective faction leaders. Second, presenting the evidence and identifying the levels of command or influence which could affect the situation proved the more challenging task. Staff officers, UNMOs, civilian officials, media conferences and external mediators were all used in numerous attempts to stop the shooting. Many met with local successes, usually short-lived.

The UN could not seem to provide sufficient incentives, nor impose sufficient costs to stop sniping and indirect fire. Indeed, this is related to the larger problem of returning Bosnia to the rule of law, in which a party identified as the perpetrator of a premeditated attack on civilians could be fairly tried in a civil court. Compare the situation in Sarajevo to the situation in the buffer zone in Cyprus, where civilian police investigated a stray shot, presented the evidence to one side, which promptly charged and imprisoned the soldier responsible for it.[35]

Campaigns to Reduce Seizures and Restrictions

Hostage-taking, seizures of personnel, personal intimidation and routine restrictions to freedom of movement severely hamper the ability of a UN force to operate. Although these incidents have occurred in other missions, such as UNTAC and ONUC, they have been most persistent and pervasive in UNPROFOR, and are indicative of the lower level of consent and cooperation faced by that mission than others.

Sarajevo Seizures

In 1993 a series of shelling incidents caused the evacuation of an UNMO house in the suburbs of Sarajevo. The evacuation was to be conducted by UNPROFOR troops with armoured vehicles, and was coordinated at sector level to ensure safe passage through the opposing force brigade area of operations. On the return trip, however, the convoy strayed into an area controlled by a local "warlord," over whom none of the factions claimed to exercise control. The vehicles were halted and forced open. Vehicles, weapons and equipment were confiscated. UNMOs escaped with most of their equipment (flak vests, binoculars, radios) by refusing to hand it over, despite being unarmed. The armed escort, however, was stripped of personal equipment, small arms, and all items of value. The soldiers and UNMOs were returned unharmed to UNPROFOR lines.[36]

Attempts were made through both military and political channels to secure the return of vehicles and equipment, which UNPROFOR referred to as "stolen." Three days later the vehicles and some items of equipment were returned (possibly in exchange for fuel). Some observers credited the weak and delayed UN response with encouraging subsequent hijack and theft attempts. A few days later, for example, a different faction halted a convoy from the same UN contingent, forced open the doors and seized several protected persons, who were threatened with execution. Rapid escalation to the political level and threats of international publicity secured the release of the protected persons. In this case, it was clear that political authorities were in control of the military faction, while in the case of the earlier seizure, the "warlord's" faction was not responsive to political pressure.

As a postscript to these two events, local authorities subsequently attacked and defeated the rogue "warlord" responsible for the earlier hijacking, and tried and imprisoned a leader for criminal activity. Observers interpreted this as a sign that the rogue faction had ceased to serve any common interests, and had become an embarrassment to the established government.

Firepower Demonstration at Maslenica Bridge

In 1993, CANBAT 1 was moved from the quiet Sector West to the less tranquil Sector South in the area overlooking the Maslenica Bridge. The battalion they were replacing had been subject to frequent intimidation, restriction of movement on roads, restraint of soldiers in OPs and quarters, and periodic shelling. In one incident, an OP clearly flying the UN flag was repeatedly shelled in what was construed as a clear attempt to intimidate its occupants.

One of the factions felt that they had a clear superiority in equipment; they had tanks, and had been very dismissive of the Canadian M113 armoured personnel carriers. In order to establish an effective working relationship in the new area, the commanding officer arranged a firepower demonstration of the TOW-under-armour vehicles in his battalion anti-armour platoon. The demonstration was set up in an area which could be observed, and the local commanders were invited. Tank hulks well beyond the range of tank guns were selected and the TOW vehicles fired from concealed positions in defilade. At least one of the targets had been prepared to explode impressively. The demonstration of TOW capabilities was billed as a training activity, of professional interest to opposing commanders, but the clear message was that tanks would not come out of a confrontation well. The message was reinforced by professional discussions surrounding the firepower demonstration.

Assessment of Campaign Factors

These incidents occurred in quite different contexts. The first Sarajevo seizure was the work of a rogue faction which was not responsive to political pressure. Without the direct use of force, either in self-defence or retaliation, there was no pressure which could be brought to bear to secure the return of stolen weapons and equipment. Since the motivation was mainly pecuniary, any offer to buy back the equipment would likely stimulate further hijackings. The second seizure, however, was by a faction responsive to political pressure and release was secured by escalating the negotiations quickly to the highest level. In this case, there was no gain from the hijacking, but nor was there a disincentive to further direct action.

Any situation which places valuable assets in the hands of unprincipled factions not subject to a chain of command demands a combat response. This was eventually taken by a government anxious to demonstrate its legitimacy and control of the area, rather than by the UN. Desire for legitimacy was also the main lever used on the other faction to secure release of protected persons in the case of the second seizure mentioned.

In contrast, the firepower demonstration was an explicit use of combat power to influence the calculations of a comparatively coherent chain of command. It was coupled with the unequivocal message (delivered in meetings at company and battalion level) that trained professional soldiers with effective weapons would use active force to defend themselves and their mandate against any threat. This clarity of communication, both through contact and the orchestrated display of combat power, is credited with reducing the number of restriction and intimidation incidents experienced by CANBAT 1, and assisting it subsequently in the execution of the Medak pocket operation (described below).

Campaigns to Prevent Armed Incursion

It is easier to prevent an armed incursion than to reverse it. This is demonstrated by a comparison of the Croatian incursions along the Zagreb-Belgrade highway in January 1993 and in the Medak pocket in September 1993. The origin of the attacks was the ambiguity of the Vance plan, referred to above. The outcome of the two operations was comparable—a comparatively secure buffer zone. The progress of the two incidents, however, was very different.

Blocking the Croatian Advance into the Krajina

As a result of an impasse at the strategic level, Croatian forces advanced to seize control of areas within Croatian territory on 22 January 1993. Had there been more warning, diplomatic channels might have been used to pressure Croatia. As it was, political officers and liaison officers alike were caught flat-footed.[37] The advance gained control of parts of the Moslavaka plateau, the Maslenica Bridge, Zemunic airfield, and the Peruka dam. Along the Zagreb-Belgrade highway, however, they encountered prepared UN positions. Near Novska, two companies occupied dug-in positions with all-round defence and heavy weapons covering a narrow avenue of advance. This imposed a pause, presumably while commanders in Zagreb weighed the costs and advantages of pushing through the UN positions.

Both military liaison officers in Zagreb and political officers attached to the force and sector headquarters used this delay to meet with counterparts at brigade level and higher. Every opportunity was taken to stress the preparedness of the positions and the determination of the UN forces to hold them against attack from *either* side. At the same time, hope was held out for a diplomatic resolution, involving closer UN supervision of the implementation of an agreement.[38]

The determined stand with a viable defensive option at the tactical level was reinforced by liaison and negotiation at the operational level which emphasized the UN position, leaving no margin of doubt about the response to an attack. Negotiations at the highest level were able to capitalize on this; Croatian officers in the field fed information to their superiors which confirmed the UN's determined stance at a higher level. In this case the territory lost to the buffer zone was minimal.

Retaking the Medak Pocket

On 9 September 1993 Croatian forces launched a surprise attack on Serb positions in the area of Medak, gaining a large pocket of territory which had been occupied by Serb civilians. Serbs retaliated with artillery attacks on Karlovac and a FROG missile attack on Zagreb. On 13 September, Croatian authorities in Zagreb agreed to return to the 9 September demarcation line. UN forces were to implement the Medak Pocket Agreement by separating the opposing forces, supervising the withdrawal of Croatian forces to the 9 September line, and establishing an UNPROFOR controlled demilitarized buffer zone between Serb and Croat forces.

The UN battalion commander planned a four-phase operation. First, two companies would replace the Serbs in their front line positions. UNMOs on the Croatian side were to confirm the location of the pre-9 September lines to which Croatian forces were to withdraw. Second, a crossing-point on the main road would be opened between the Serbian and Croatian frontline positions. The anti-armour platoon would provide overwatch with TOW-under-armour (TUA) vehicles, outranging any tanks in use by either side. Engineers were tasked with mine-clearance. Third, two companies would cross to the Croatian side, where one would occupy the frontline positions in contact. The other company would move to the back of the pocket and secure the Croatian frontline positions of 9 September, to which the Croatian forces were to have withdrawn. The final phase was to ensure that all Croatian forces withdrew to the pre 9 September line. Patrolling tasks would commence in the buffer zone, and teams would assist UNHCR and UN Civil Affairs in the provision of relief, identification of dead and so on.

The operation commenced 15 September 1993 with the occupation of Serb positions. Direct liaison had been established with local Serb commanders, because the UN force was moving up through their area. Serb forces then withdrew to the agreed line. Upon assuming positions in the front line, UN forces came under machine gun, mortar and 20 mm cannon fire from Croatian forces. The UN responded to fire in kind: small arms for small arms, .50 calibre heavy machine gun for 20 mm and so on. As the fire fight continued and increased in intensity, the UN commander began to suspect that the Croatian Military Command had not informed their soldiers that a cease-fire agreement was being implemented. He could not cross into Croatian lines, nor could liaison officers or UNMOs with the Croatian Military Command confirm that the information had been passed to troops in the front lines.

Eventually a meeting was arranged at Gospić during the evening of 15 September at which the Croatian operational zone commander agreed to permit the crossing point to be established during the night of 15-16 September, and crossing to begin not earlier than 1200 hours on 16 September. Part of the reason for the delay was to ensure that all Croatian forces got proper notification of the cease-fire and withdrawal agreement; this had been a problem with other cease-fires. The key people attending this meeting were the UN battalion commander, the Chief Operations Officer of UNPROFOR, and the Senior Military Observer of Sector South. On the Croatian side, it was the operational zone commander who had the authority to arrange the crossing and Croatian withdrawal.

Commencing at first light, troops in contact reported explosions, small arms fire, and smoke from villages, indicating action being taken against the local civilian population. The UN force was not permitted to cross into the Medak pocket until 1200 hours, and the crossing point was in any case held in force against them. By the time UN forces crossed into the pocket at 1200 hours 16 September, all villages and buildings had been destroyed and there was no sign of the civilian population. Croatian forces withdrew from the area ahead of UN forces, reaching the 9 September line by 1800 hours 17 September. During 17-18 September, there were numerous minor confrontations between UN and Croatian forces as the boundaries of the demilitarized zone were established. These normally entailed Croatian threats to shoot UN patrols, and UN insistence on right of passage. On 22 September, UN and Croatian authorities signed a map agreeing to the boundaries of the buffer zone.

Assessment of Campaign Factors

The January 1993 attack occurred in the context of uncertain status differences. When the situation at the tactical level was clarified (the Zagreb-Belgrade highway would not be surrendered without a fight) then change of goals allowed comparatively rapid de-escalation of the situation in this area, but not in others. The physical attack involved the potential for direct contact, but this was largely avoided through the use of UNMOs and liaison officers between formations and the sector headquarters. Knowledge of opposing forces' movements was incomplete, but it was possible to convey the impression of UN resolve through visible preparations revealed to visitors, officers attending meetings, and media representatives. One of the most important factors in avoiding violence was the comparatively coherent chain of command and the control exerted over local forces.

The assault on the Medak pocket occurred in the context of festering resentment and what was perceived to be a long and injurious stalemate (some participants dated it from the Vance accord). Having representatives of both Sector South (the Senior UNMO) and UNPROFOR (the Chief of Staff) located forward at the key headquarters in Gospić was a crucial step in expediting effective communications; it prevented the UN hierarchy from being manipulated to delay the operation. After the operation, a special negotiating cell was formed within UNPROFOR headquarters, consisting of a general officer, two colonels, a secretary and translator support. This cell was able to provide another level of escalation above the Sector South headquarters in Knin, which had previously borne the brunt of negotiations with the Krajina Serbs.

Again, a change of goals was required before the situation in the Medak pocket could be de-escalated. In the Medak pocket, the failure of communications between Zagreb authorities and field commanders meant that this change of goals was not immediately translated into a change of behaviour. There remains an incomplete loop of accountability between Zagreb and the field commanders for the events which occurred in the Medak pocket, although indicators point to an operation which was planned and conducted at least at brigade level.

The question of UN priorities arose in the case of the Medak pocket operation. UNMOs on both sides of the line had been placed under operational control of the battalion executing the operation, and were instrumental in establishing the communications links which permitted withdrawal of Croatian forces and establishment of the buffer zone. An UNPROFOR negotiating team was also involved in negotiating the cease-fire. Bearing in mind that the battalion commander had become "decisively engaged" when the Croatian forces first refused to withdraw, it was the UNPROFOR negotiating team which made the arrangements for the crossing point to open at 1200 hours on 16 September, allowing 12 hours freedom of action for Croatian troops behind their front lines before the UN battalion's advance. Was the UN priority the preservation of a negotiated agreement to include the 1200 hours time line, or the protection of lives and property which might be endangered by adhering to the time line. In the absence of concrete information about the activities going on behind Croatian lines, the UN position was to stick to the agreed time line.[39] With the benefit of hindsight, helicopters, UNMOs, or reconnaissance in force might have been used to verify suspicions of ethnic cleansing; however, any of these actions may have caused a deterioration in the situation.

Both the January defence of the Zagreb-Belgrade highway and the September recapture of an occupied area illustrate the importance of force deployment as part of a negotiating strategy. Being in place in advance of a threat across a buffer zone is a less costly means of deterring aggressive use of force by belligerents. Having commanders forward and in contact is also as important in peacekeeping as in war.

Campaigns to Disengage

One of the first requirements of de-escalation is to separate belligerents, and campaigns for disengagement and withdrawal are a consistent feature of peacekeeping operations. They have sometimes been dealt with in terms of lines of operation as part of a campaign strategy.[40] Two examples of disengagement illustrate the difference between a "bottom-up" process taking advantage of exhaustion and a "top-down" process which executes a strategic agreement.

A "Gentlemen's Agreement"

In October 1993, a series of reactive shooting incidents erupted in Bosnia with each faction blaming the others and retaliating. By travelling hundreds of kilometers, Commander Sector South was able to visit each of the commanders, and discuss the causes and potential for a cease-fire. They were all receptive to the idea of a cease-fire, but each distrusted the others. On 29 October he sent the same letter to each of the key commanders, requesting a cease-fire effective from noon three days hence. The cease-fire was initially for only one week, and was ostensibly linked to the International Commission on the Former Yugoslavia (ICFY) negotiations then in progress.[41]

The cease-fire became known as the "gentlemen's agreement" and lasted through to the following spring with few violations. Under the cover of the cease-fire a number of other initiatives and confidence building measures were attempted, some with success.

While the "gentlemen's agreement" was still in effect, a small contingent of Croatian troops was trapped on the Trlo Ridge. A stalemate ensued in which one side was unwilling to attack to remove the incursion and the other was unwilling to attack to extract them. Both sides shelled neighbouring villages. Repeated attempts by the UN to verify the incursion were prevented by both sides. Eventually one side requested UN protection to evacuate its troops, ending the shelling by both sides to mutual advantage. This was stalled for weeks. Finally the ridge was abandoned to UN supervision at the end of March, after almost a month.

Establishing the Mostar and Tuzla Buffer Zones

The establishment of buffer zones around Mostar and Tuzla in Bosnia was not the result of local initiatives, but a consequence of the Washington Accords, which made provision for the separation of forces. The execution of this was left to sector level, which delegated the operation to battalions in the areas affected. UNMOs were placed under operational control for liaison, and were in place prior to the first reconnaissance. They were followed by company and battalion level liaison officers attached to both sides. The commanding officers drove and walked the line of separation, and negotiated with local commanders to maximize the separation between forces. Initially, forces were reluctant to withdraw from the line of demarcation. Only with the arrival of UN forces and the establishment of observation posts and patrol tracks did each side begin the withdrawal to the agreed distance. It was not possible to achieve separation beyond line-of-sight and small-arms range in all cases.

Reconnaissance had been conducted by UN units down to platoon level, and liaison was established immediately to avoid misunderstanding. The most delicate time was the period of the actual insertion of UN forces and mutual withdrawal of combatants. The commanding officer was forward at the point of contact, accompanied by one of the belligerent commanders and a liaison officer from the other side. This group moved as a "fire brigade" to resolve immediately any difficulties which could not be handled by liaison at lower levels.[42]

The Mostar and Tuzla defenders, as the weaker parties, were most anxious to see the peacekeepers arrive. Care had to be taken to avoid the impression that the UN was coming to their rescue; observation posts had to be sited with the approval of both sides, and efforts were made to assure those outside the line that the force would function to prevent attacks *out of* as well as *into* the area.[43]

Assessment of Campaign Factors

In both cases, the context of the conflict shifted to permit de-escalation. By late October 1993, mutual exhaustion and the need for an operational pause was driving the calculations of many of the local commanders. Commander Sector South was able to take advantage of this. The wide dispersion of forces meant that small engagements could, and probably did, continue at various times without the overall cease-fire being jeopardized. In neither of the cases was the control over militia absolute, although the chain of command was sufficiently in control to deliver for the first crucial week of the "gentlemen's agreement." The long lead time (three days) had been specifically calculated to allow time for all factions to notify their fighters, and to be personally contacted by the local UN commander or observer.

The Mostar and Tuzla cases present interesting examples of multi-party meetings. It is generally acknowledged that the more people in a meeting, the harder it is to get agreement. Many experienced negotiators have commented on the increasing difficulty of arranging concessions in public forums.[44] The withdrawal of Croatian Guard and JNA forces from the UNPAs in 1992 was arranged in small and almost clandestine meetings.[45] While the key details and concessions were arranged in small, usually bilateral meetings, multi-party meetings were useful in cementing deals and demonstrating confidence to all the military and civilian parties involved. Setting up and orchestrating multi-party meetings was a drain on the staff, and required considerable diplomacy of the chairman (usually the battalion commander) and the interpreters.

The gentleman's agreement, on the other hand, represents "go-between" mediation at its most exacting: dealing with intransigent and changeable negotiators separated by hundreds of kilometers of bad roads, poor communications, bad weather, and interminable checkpoints:

> Following nineteen meetings and 2500 kilometers in my trusty 4x4
> in four days, exasperation led me to declare that through my so far
> fruitless efforts I was demonstrating greater concern for the safety of
> the civilians than the two brothers were. Eureka! The shooting stops
> and stays stopped and negotiations become more fruitful. I later
> became convinced that our earnest efforts then and before, efforts
> known to be in the interests of both sides, efforts greater than their
> own, efforts in danger of becoming known as such and as ours alone,
> caused these brothers to stop killing each others' families in this
> instance. . . .[46]

I conclude the case studies with this observation because it illustrates another of the roles of the third party in initiating de-escalation. Commander Sector South is describing a subtle attitude shift which is brought about almost entirely as a result of external intervention. This shift must be pushed beyond the initial defensive stages of stopping the shooting and moving, and extended to encompass cooperation for mutual benefit.

Observations About Dealing With Coercive Force

In each of the situations above, UN forces had to deal with armed coercion, often in defiance of various agreements with the factions. Sniping violated cease-fires; indirect fire violated both cease-fires and (frequently) heavy weapons bans; restrictions and kidnappings violate the rather loose status of forces agreement (loose because not all the parties have signed it); the fighting in the Medak pocket was in defiance of an agreement to withdraw. Effective handling of incidents would reinforce the agreements, and reduce the likelihood of further incidents.

How Do You Deal With Coercion?

In looking for effective campaign strategies, one starting point is the literature on handling coercion in negotiations. Fisher and Ury address the problem of dealing with "dirty tricks" in Getting to Yes. If they use dirty tricks, negotiate the rules of the game. If they present phoney facts, insist on verifying them. If their authority is ambiguous or their intentions dubious, do not negotiate until you have verified the status of the negotiations. Reject the psychological warfare of stressful situations, personal attacks, and positional pressure tactics.[47]

But board-room negotiation in which the communication is exclusively through "contact" is a far cry from peacekeeping operations in which combat and coercive force form a routine part of communications. In peacekeeping there is a basic principle for de-escalating coercive situations. The principle, developed by Ben Hoffman of the Canadian International Institute for Negotiation, is "four-fifths-of-a-tit-for-a-tat."

First, the context of communication is important in responding to coercion. As indicated by the case studies above, "Parties assess their relative power in choosing whether to accommodate, collaborate, or withdraw."[48] The outcome of the incident

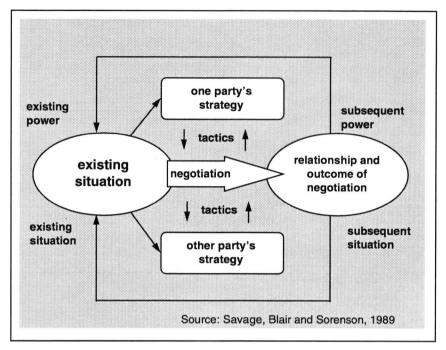

Figure 16: Context of Negotiations

will affect subsequent power relationships and perceptions, which will affect subsequent conflicts. The process is illustrated in Figure 16. This is why weak tactics tend to be counter-productive when facing coercion. They actually encourage subsequent attempts at coercive negotiation.

For soldiers, this is a blinding flash of the obvious. However, peacekeepers are also painfully aware that they often bargain from a position of real weakness. There are many stories of mission-oriented convoy leaders and local commanders who have bought their way through roadblocks with fuel "taxes" or other minor breaches of expected UN conduct only to see both tolls and delays rise inexorably.[49]

Second, the nature of coercive situations conditions the response. Since there are situations which do not lend themselves to direct negotiation, what posture on the ground is most conducive to effective indirect negotiations, and subsequent linkage to compliance? The short answer is a robust and defensible posture. The Sarajevo seizures, in which higher commanders and staffs were scrabbling to save soldiers taken hostage is precisely the sort of situation one wants to avoid, if opposing forces are to be edged towards compliance. The more effective the local defence and security of troops using combat techniques, the greater the scope for innovative and daring contact skills.

Third, the nature of the parties influences the intervention strategy. The less coherent the chain of command, the less the scope for influencing belligerent behaviour over time. The corollary to this is that the more breaks there are (or purport to be) in the chain of command, the more labour-intensive communications become. If you can be sure that something communicated to the Brigade headquarters will be transmitted quickly and efficiently to all ranks, then one liaison officer at brigade level will do; if not, liaison officers may have to be placed with subordinate commanders.

Strategy To Resist Coercion — "Four-Fifths-Of-A-Tit-For-A-Tat"

How should peacekeepers deal with coercive force? The traditional guideline has been "firm, fair and friendly" and this comes remarkably close to describing the most effective way of dealing with attempts at physical coercion. The "four-fifths-of-a-tit-for-a-tat" rule was developed by Ben Hoffman of the Canadian International Institute of Applied Negotiation. It suggests four steps:

1. Always lead with a cooperative gesture.

2. Be alive to feed-back from the opposition.

3. Punish coercive behaviour. At least, do not reward coercive behaviour.

4. Offer conciliation as a reward for de-escalation.

This strategy is derived from an adaptation of the "tit-for-tat" strategy, which rewards cooperation with cooperation, and punishes coercion with coercion. Tit-for-tat is probably the most common "game strategy" seen in peacekeeping operations. As peacekeepers are aware, it tends to be escalatory, because of the dynamics of perception in protracted social conflict. A player perceives the opponent's "tat" as worse than his own "tit"—each iteration tends towards further escalation.

The "four-fifths-of-a-tit-for-a-tat" strategy offsets this tendency to escalate by starting with conciliation, responding in kind to conciliatory overtures, and consistently resisting coercion. What would it look like in practice? The Medak pocket operation probably illustrates a practical application. The careful negotiation and liaison prior to the advance of UN troops was an exercise in cooperation. When opposition was met on the Croatian front lines, white vehicles advanced with blue flags flying, clearly visible. When shooting started, fire was returned in kind—small-arms for small-arms, HMG for HMG. There was no withdrawal. Subsequent meetings offered a way out of the impasse with a new time line which preserved all the features of the original agreement of 13 September.

Force Level Operations and De-escalation Strategy

All peacekeeping operations exist in a larger context, and the de-escalation of local violence is only part of the task facing commanders and staffs at force headquarters. Their mandate stops at the borders of the affected area, but the "grand strategy" of the UN and regional organizations links the mandate to the maintenance of regional stability.

UNIFIL and UNFICYP derive their longevity from the consequences of failure to contain a conflict: a wider war involving the Middle East or Greece and Turkey would be a serious blow to international security. The problem is that de-escalation of the conflict from violence to segregation (according to Figure 3 in Chapter Two) has stifled all further attempts to de-escalate the conflict further, despite the potential to do so. The long-term costs of missions like UNFICYP are lightly borne, in comparison to the costs of a major regional war, but are still heavy compared to the "opportunity cost" represented by not having a healthy and productive region free of protracted social conflict.

The former Yugoslavia presents a far greater threat if conflict spreads to neighbouring countries than if violence can be contained within Yugoslavia's former borders. In this it is like Cyprus and Lebanon. A strategy of "concentric containment" has been described by Andrew Bair, a former political officer with the force. The strategy consists of an outer ring of preventive deployment (UN forces in Macedonia) and preventive diplomacy within the framework of both the UN and regional organizations (OSCE, NATO, and WEU). The middle ring consists of strengthening the UN Protected Areas and buffer zones. The inner ring is described as military stabilization in Bosnia.[50]

The containment strategy is essentially defensive. To rely only on the military contribution to stability inside the theatre is to miss the opportunity to push de-escalation past the current defensive stalemate and take on some of the causes of the conflict at community level. The prerequisite for this is a stable and secure environment within which civilian groups can operate across communal boundaries.

Conclusions

This chapter has addressed questions about planning campaigns for the de-escalation of violence at the operational and tactical level. It described the relationship between handling of incidents and linking of incidents, and gave examples of the way in which the context, conflict and parties involved influence the intervention strategy. Two questions were posed at the outset about the coordination of de-escalation campaigns. How are contact and combat skills orchestrated to achieve de-escalation? And what opportunities are there for "offensive" action against the roots of the conflict, by military forces?

Orchestration of Combat and Contact Skills

At least five useful conclusions can be drawn about the orchestration of combat and contact skills.

First, combat capability and force deployment is an essential element of a negotiating strategy. Forces must be deployed in ways which minimize their vulnerability, lest they subsequently become an opposing force asset in the negotiation process.

Second, commanders or staff who become "decisively engaged" in a confrontation are no longer in a position to de-escalate it, and the negotiation must be shifted to a higher level for resolution. In more fluid situations, or where there is an unclear chain of command, contact might be shifted laterally or to a new agent. When the negotiation shifts, the troops in place should be able to provide the stability and security necessary to permit the situation to be viewed dispassionately at the next level. This is not to say that situations are automatically escalated. Competent peacekeepers will always resolve incidents at the lowest possible level.

Third, when a negotiation is escalated or shifted, the setting should be changed to distance it from obstructions to settlement inherent in the former situation. This applies equally at the tactical and operational level. Preventing further incidents to disrupt negotiations is generally a combat function.

Fourth, the de-escalation campaign must address the sources or causes of incidents, which may not always be apparent where they occur. Forces in contact are unlikely to be able to determine these without staff and multi-agency assistance. It is this element of the de-escalation process that necessitates "offensive" action which may be economic and social rather than military, and may fit into a longer timescale than the immediate military operation. Offensive action will therefore normally involve civilian agencies.

Finally, the "four-fifths-of-a-tit-for-a-tat" strategy provides a simple guideline for de-escalation when faced with coercion. Unfortunately, in its military context, it requires a capability which peacekeeping forces do not always possess relative to the belligerents.

Opportunities for Offensive Action

The nature of de-escalation limits the contribution that can be made by military peacekeepers. Soldiers are not well equipped for the gradual, long-term transformation of attitudes necessary to undermine inter-communal hatred. Nevertheless, the case studies and interviews suggest at least four opportunities for offensive action by military peacekeepers.

First, every meeting can be an opportunity to stifle the invective of hate which has an escalatory dynamic of its own. While each side is entitled to repeat its own version of history, (or "apocrypha" as it has been called) unfounded statements, hyperbole and malice can be excised from negotiations. Military negotiators can insist that their counterparts deal honestly with today's problems, to build relationships for tomorrow.

Second, any military action which reinforces the coherence and reliability of the belligerents' chain of command, or the responsiveness of factions to higher authority, is likely to make it easier to deal with factions in the future. The liaison and negotiation system permits this by building up relationships at multiple points in the hierarchy on both sides of a confrontation line. Nurturing and reinforcing the live-and-let-live system can lead to an expansion into civilian life and inter-communal contacts, if military peacekeepers work closely with local civilians and civilian third parties.

Third, it is sometimes necessary for the military third party to "run interference" to protect local arrangements from deliberate sabotage by central authorities. This may run counter to the second opportunity. Coherent chains of command prevent rogue violence, but can also be used to undermine the evolution of a live-and-let-live system. Local tranquillity can easily be sacrificed to higher objectives. When this threatens, military third parties may be able to bring pressure to bear to prevent local progress from being derailed.

Finally, soldiers can build a broad understanding that neighbouring communities are mutually dependent for lasting security. The critical milestone for this opportunity is the ability of the third party to bring together people from each side on a regular basis. Once sufficient security, stability and confidence has been achieved to permit this, then advanced contact skills can usefully be employed, and civilians can continue the offensive against the conflict.

Endnotes

1   After Major-General Clive Milner succeeded in demilitarizing the portion of the Buffer Zone, over which the Greek- and Turk-Cypriot forces faced each other at very close quarters, this sort of incident became much rarer.

2   Major-General Lewis MacKenzie, Peacekeeper: The Road to Sarajevo (Toronto: Douglas and McIntyre, 1993), 45.

3   Front page stories from a variety of Cyprus papers between February and April 1989 include the following progressively more negative reports: on 6 February Simerini warned of a Turkish trap; on 2 March Agon claimed that the agreements were failing through Turkish fault; on 5 March, President Clerides chastised the press for its unproductive fuss; on 31 March, Elephtherotypia accused the President of secret moves; on 1 April Kirikas claimed that new American proposals were a dangerous fraud; and on 5 April, the Cyprus Mail reported that the disengagement plan favoured the Turkish side.

4   Elias Canetti, Crowds and Power, (Harmondsworth: Penguin, 1960), 119: "...a few single men are killed: only the deaths caused by the *other* side are really noticed. From this moment on, an unshakeable conviction reigns that the enemy want to exterminate the whole tribe ..."

5   Robert D. Kaplan, Balkan Ghosts: A Journey Through History, (New York: Vintage Books, 1993), xvii.

6   D. M. Last, "Peacekeeping Doctrine and Conflict Resolution Techniques," Armed Forces and Society 22:2 (Winter 1995/1996) pp. 187-210. Over the period 1986 to 1992, a comparatively tranquil period, the Canadian sector experienced an average of 38 incidents per month. An average of four meetings a month were recorded at company and battalion level (more meetings were held, but only a certain number warranted minutes). Linear regression of "incidents reported" on "meetings recorded" yields an r^2 value of .305; suspected reasons are discussed in the reference.

7   These generalizations are drawn almost exclusively from Canadian sources and may not be applicable to other national contingents, although anecdotes suggest that they may be. For the prescriptive sequence of negotiations, in addition to the material discussed in Chapter Three, see the Peacekeeper's Handbook, 117-119; Nordic UN Tactical Manual, 70-73; Joint Task Force Commander's Handbook for Peace Operations, 46-51; Russian manual, UN Peacekeeping

Operations: Organization, Conduct and Logistics Functional Duties of Personnel, 103-107; Canadian manual, Operations Land and Tactical Air, Volume 3: Peacekeeping Operations, 7-8-4 to 7-8-6, the British manual, Army Field Manual Volume V: All Arms Tactics, Special Operations and Techniques Part 1 Peacekeeping Operations, 7-8 to 7-12, and the American manual, FM 100-23 Peace Operations, 2, 5, 6, 34 and 39. The consistency of the prescriptive guidelines for negotiation suggests that all of the above manuals owe a certain debt to the original International Peace Academy version of the Peacekeeper's Handbook. There is more variation in practice because of personalities and experience, but the scope for invention is not limitless.

8   Interview with a Canadian officer, March 1994.

9   Canadian Broadcasting Corporation, "Sniper," CBC Sunday Morning, (27 February 1994).

10 Interview with a Canadian officer on 18 March 1994 at Ottawa concerning events in UNPROFOR in September 1993.

11 Interview with a Canadian officer on 28 February 1995 at Leavenworth, concerning events in the Sarajevo area, UNPROFOR, Summer 1994.

12 Interview with an American officer on 30 March 1995 at Fort Leavenworth concerning events in UNPROFOR in 1994.

13 Numerous interviews attest to this. It is also referred to in "Convoy Operations," Dispatches: The Army's Lessons Learned Newsletter, 1:1 (November 1994).

14 Interview with a Canadian officer on 1 March 1995 at Fort Leavenworth concerning events in UNPROFOR in September 1994.

15 See Last, op. cit.

16 "...direct truces were easily suppressed. Orders were issued ..." Robert Axelrod, The Evolution of Cooperation (New York: Basic Books, 1984), 78.

17 Tony Ashworth, Trench Warfare, 1914-1918: The Live and Let Live System (New York: Holmes and Meier, 1980), 169.

18 Interview with an American officer on 30 March at Fort Leavenworth concerning events in UNPROFOR in summer 1994.

19 Interview with two Canadian officers, on 28 February 1995 at Fort Leavenworth and on 15 May 1993 at Camp Wainwright, Alberta concerning events in Sector West, March 1993.

20 See D. M. Last "Cooperation between Units and Observers," Peacekeeping and International Relations, 23:5 (September-October 1994), 4.

21 Andrew Bair, "What Happened in Yugoslavia? Lessons for Future Peacekeepers," European Security, 3:2 (Summer 1994), 346.

22 Interview with an UNMO in May 1994 at Split concerning events in UNPROFOR.

23 Derived from sources cited by Dennis J. D. Sandole, "Paradigms, theories and metaphors in conflict and conflict resolution: Coherence or confusion?" and Daniel Druckman, "An Analytical Research Agenda for Conflict and Conflict Resolution," in Conflict Resolution Theory and Practice: Integration and Application, edited by Dennis J. D. Sandole and Hugo van der Merwe (New York: Manchester University Press, 1993).

24 Interview with Ms. Dolores B. Lasan, Chief of Mission, UNHCR in Cyprus, February 1993 at Nicosia, Cyprus.

25 Interview with a Canadian officer in March 1994 at Ottawa concerning events in UNIFIL and UNTSO, in 1985 which he observed as a UNMO.

26 Jonathan Bendor, "Uncertainty and the Evolution of Cooperation," Journal of Conflict Resolution (1993).

27 G. H. Greenwell, An Infant in Arms (London: Allen Lane, 1972), 17, cited by Axelrod, 80.

28 Bair, op. cit., 343.

29 Interviews with two British officers at Fort Leavenworth concerning events in UNPROFOR in 1993 and 1994.

30 Interview with a Canadian officer on 28 February 1995, and with an American officer on 26 March 1995 at Fort Leavenworth concerning events in UNPROFOR in 1994.

31 Interview with a Canadian officer on 9 March 1995 at Ottawa concerning events in UNPROFOR in 1992-1993.

32 Ibid.

33 Interview with a Canadian officer on 28 February 1995, and with an American officer on 26 March 1995 at Fort Leavenworth concerning events in UNPROFOR in 1994.

34 Mr. Melita Richter Malabotta, "The Balkan Irrationalities," Paper presented at the Freidrich Naumann Foundation and the Janus Pannonius University International Conference on Reasons and Consequences of the Crisis in the Former Yugoslavia, (Pécs, Hungary: 1-4 December 1994), 14.

35 Last, "Peacekeeping Doctrine and Conflict Resolution Techniques," op. cit.

36 Interview with a Canadian officer.

37 Bair, 348.

38 Interviews with three Canadian officers concerning the same events in UNPROFOR.

39 Interview with a former commanding officer and draft CANBAT 1 Report on Medak Pocket Operations15-21 September 1993.

40 Major Walter E. Kretchik, "Peacemaking and Operational Art: The Israeli Experience in Operation 'Peace for Galilee'" (Fort Leavenworth: School of Advanced Military Studies Monograph, 1992) argues, based on Operation "Peace for Galilee", that operational art can be used to design and explain a peacemaking campaign, but will not guarantee success. Major Victor M. Robertson, "The Relationship Between War and Peacekeeping," (Fort Leavenworth: School of Advanced Military Studies Monograph, 1992) "The critical operational design issues are where the zone should be, and where the force commander should place his troops in the zone...", 19.

41 Interview with a former Sector Commander. Related documents provided by staff officers.

42 Interview with a former commanding officer, May 1994, at Split concerning events in Sector South in 1994.

43 Interview with a senior UNMO in May 1994 at Dubrovnik concerning events in Sector South, UNPROFOR in which he participated as an UNMO and Senior UNMO.

44 Interviews, Major Barry Taylor, Lieutenant Colonel Davidson, Captain Lloyd Chubbs.

45 Commanders were smuggled across lines in UN vehicles in the early stages. Interview with Major Barry Taylor in October 1993 at St. Hubert, concerning events in UNPROFOR Sector West in 1992 and 1993 which he observed as a G3 staff officer.

46 Colonel G. J. Oehring, "Between Brothers: Some Views from a Year in Croatia," unpublished paper, 4.

47 Roger Fisher, William Ury and Bruce Patton, Getting to Yes: Negotiating Agreement Without Giving In, 2d ed., (Toronto: Penguin, 1991), summary of related points appears on 194-5.

48 Grant T. Savage, John D. Blair and Ritch L. Sorenson, "Consider Both Relationships and Substance When Negotiating Strategically," in Negotiation: Readings, Exercises and Cases, 2d ed., edited by Roy J. Lewicki, Joseph A. Litterer, David M. Saunders and John W. Minton (Boston: Irwin, 1993), 57.

49 Interviews with Canadian liaison officers in Sector South, UNPROFOR, March 1994.

50 Andrew S. Bair, "Managing the Crisis in the Former Yugoslavia," in Peace Support Operations and the U.S. Military, edited by Dennis J. Quinn (Washington, DC: Institute for National Strategic Studies, 1994), 217-233.

Chapter Six

Winning the Peace

Do you know, Fantanes, what astonishes me most in this world?
The inability of force to create anything. In the long run, the sword
is always beaten by the spirit.[1]

Napoleon

This study has addressed de-escalation of violence, which comprises the operational art of peacekeeping. It builds on the pioneering work of Ron Fisher, Betts Fetherston, and others who have linked peacekeeping practice to conflict resolution theory. It goes further to link theory and evolving military doctrine to the practical business of stopping belligerents from firing and moving against each other.

Stopping the shooting and moving, however, is only the beginning. Controlling military violence is a defensive function which cannot win the peace. Rebuilding the trust and mutual confidence of erstwhile enemies, undermining the causes of conflict, and ending mutual hate and fear constitute offensive action. Soldiers play an important role in offensive action against conflict, because of the security guarantees they can provide and the common culture and understanding between soldiers. Nevertheless, soldiers are ill-equipped to launch sustained offensives which rely on political, social and economic development over decades, even generations. Integrating civilian peace-pushing and peace-building efforts at the operational level is therefore essential to effective de-escalation.

By combining conflict resolution theory, military doctrine, and a survey of some practical peacekeeping problems, this study provides insights which help make sense out of things which peacekeepers and academics already know about, each from their own perspectives.

Theory of Conflict De-escalation

The process of making violent and potentially violent situations more benign over time is the essence of peacekeeping. Theory supported by empirical research provides signposts for the sequence of de-escalation, the basic steps required of peacekeepers, and suggests important roles for civilians in the fight against violent conflict. Theory and research which addresses relations between groups rather than models of reified state actors in a rational world should guide studies of conflict de-escalation.

Protracted Social Conflicts

Many of the situations facing peacekeepers today can be described as protracted social conflicts. These give rise to at least three distinct challenges. By undermining state power, this sort of conflict demands that peacekeepers assist in controlling the sources of violence, while settlement and eventual resolution is sought. Second, the sources of violence are more intractable and difficult to assess. Finally, many of the issues may be defined by the parties in zero-sum terms, exacerbating the problems inherent in third party intervention. For these reasons, peacekeepers face unique problems in attempting to de-escalate protracted social conflicts.

Research on the causes and correlates of inter-group violence suggests some of the actions which might be required of peacekeepers intervening in protracted social conflicts. First, physical separation of warring communities may be a necessary starting point. The psychological or social learning dimension should be addressed as early as possible, preventing the hardening of attitudes and hatreds. Economic development and political restructuring may be part of the solution; powerful factions must be acknowledged and included in the process. Group identities must be protected and given outlets which do not threaten other groups. Moderates in each community need to be protected and encouraged, and contacts maintained between communities. These contacts must be used to counter the spiral of escalating hostility which may accompany outbursts of violence.

This prescription sounds interventionist, and should not obscure the basic truth that only a solution acceptable to the belligerent communities will be durable. The prevalence of economic, social and political elements in the solution, however, demonstrates that de-escalation is not just a military task. The military role in de-escalating violence is primarily to control and prevent physical violence, creating the environment which will permit others to pursue long term solutions.

Sequence of De-escalation

The sequence of de-escalation is derived from the body of theory discussed in Chapter Two. Mitchell's dynamic protraction model of de-escalation shows how conflicts may circle back to earlier stages. The contingency model of third party intervention describes different roles at different stages in the de-escalation of a conflict. Three crucial roles for peacekeepers described by Fetherston are controlling the physical violence in a conflict, producing an atmosphere conducive to negotiations (including communications between communities) and facilitating settlement and resolution. Some of the factors which Wall has identified as conducive to de-escalation are stalemate, fatigue, yielding or changing of goals, and conciliatory gestures.

The first stage in de-escalating violent conflicts is to control them by stopping the violence. This is normally brought about with the consent of the parties in the form of a cease-fire agreement. Immediately, incentives and assurances must be offered to bring the parties to the negotiation table. These may include *disincentives* to continuing armed struggle. The "peace-pushing" phase is followed by "peace-building" which aims to build the trust and confidence between parties necessary for them to enter into binding agreements. The next phase is settlement and resolution, which is largely a diplomatic endeavour, probably requiring military support for verification, assurances, and so on. The final stage of de-escalation is post-conflict peace-building to prevent the recurrence of conditions which gave rise to violent conflict in the first place.

There are military roles in each of these phases, but the civilian and diplomatic component becomes increasingly prominent as the physical violence declines. Soldiers should be prepared to follow the lead of civilians after the initial stages.

De-escalation Techniques at the Tactical Level

The contingency model of third party intervention combines with observations from peacekeeping missions to suggest specific contact techniques which peacekeepers can use to de-escalate conflicts.

The most common of these is "constabulary intervention," in which military peacekeepers act as police to halt or deter the actions of opposing forces. As illustrated by UN forces in Cyprus, the constabulary role can be extended to maintain "rule of law" over the belligerent forces, with their active consent and cooperation. Arbitration, or the imposition of a binding judgement over belligerent forces has the effect of stifling escalation of violent incidents.

Go-between mediation allows peacekeepers to prevent misinterpretation of the other side's actions, further stifling escalating violence. Go-between mediation in a civilian context helps to keep channels of communication open between the communities; these channels become important for further de-escalation efforts.

Conciliation consists of actions and discussions to reduce the hostility each opposing force feels for the other. Conciliation is limited by a posture of armed confrontation, which emphasizes the importance of targeting education and civilian populations.

Principled negotiation and integrative negotiating techniques are applicable to all stages in the de-escalation of a conflict, and should be cultivated in staff officers and commanders. This includes separating people from the problem, focusing on interests not positions, inventing options for mutual gain, and insisting on objective criteria.

Professional consultation and problem-solving workshops may be particularly useful in solving mutual security dilemmas after initial segregation and before the links between communities atrophy. These de-escalation tasks, however, rely on advanced contact skills such as true three-party mediation, language and cultural skills which soldiers normally do not develop during short peacekeeping tours. Figure 17 illustrates the contact skills which might be most commonly associated with each stage of de-escalation identified in Chapter Two. In reality, of course, such stages and sequencing are likely to be blurred.

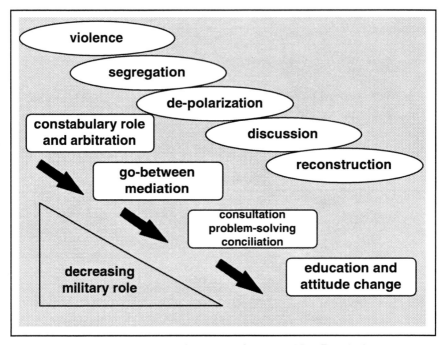

Figure 17: Contact Skills and Stages of De-Escalation

Civilian Offensive Action

The important conclusion from an examination of de-escalation techniques at the tactical level is that the "commandos" of counter-violence are more likely to be civilian than military, particularly after the shooting stops. Military forces are well equipped to handle violent situations, but less so for the long term transformations which must accompany settlement and resolution of a conflict.

Although Chapter Two offers some illustrations of consultation and conciliation in a military context, these as well as problem solving workshops, three-party mediation, education and attitude change over time must remain in the civilian domain if they are to affect the civilian populations crucial to eventual resolution of conflict.

The effectiveness of military forces in applying advanced contact skills is limited by the short duration of military rotations, and frequently by lack of language skills and specialized training in the use of contact skills. However, officers can compensate by capitalizing on the common military culture to make progress using consultation and problem solving workshops which address mainly military problems.

Civilians do more than compensate for military weaknesses. The process of conflict de-escalation beyond the purely "defensive" actions of stopping the factions from shooting and moving against each other is a fundamentally civilian process.

An important insight into the dynamics of offensive and defensive action in peacekeeping operations is that civilians lead in the offense against the roots and causes of the conflict. The greater the degree of violence from the "bottom up" the more important it is to have civilian third parties involved at the tactical level, working with the belligerent communities to rebuild trust and confidence. They do so against the background of assurances of security which initially can only be provided by peacekeepers.

Civilian offensive action is facilitated at the tactical level by defensive military action. It must also be facilitated by military and diplomatic action at the operational and strategic level. In Cyprus, both military initiatives and low level inter-communal contacts were often blocked by leaders on both sides, often for symbolic reasons. The UN mission can sometimes "run interference"—forestalling this blocking action to give low-level initiatives a chance to take root and have a positive effect. The obverse of this is that low level initiatives must be ready to exploit operational or strategic breakthroughs. When political leaders express a genuine willingness to cooperate with opposing communities, this represents a window of opportunity. Third parties at the operational and strategic level should constantly look for such openings as gestures of good faith. The right sort of security guarantee can convert such opportunities into progress which is both substantively and symbolically important.

Doctrine for De-escalation

Peacekeeping doctrine for soldiers has expanded tremendously since the Peacekeeper's Handbook was first published. Despite this, a definitive concept for the employment of peacekeeping forces has yet to emerge. Certain common principles have been widely accepted, and these underpin a theory of peacekeeping, which has been most effectively presented by Fetherston.

Applying Principles

One of the hardest principles to apply in practice has proved to be "clarity of intent". All parties, including all of the participants in the peacekeeping operation, must have a clear understanding of what the mission is trying to achieve. This common vision of the purpose and ultimate goal of the mission is necessary to unify the efforts of military, civilian, diplomatic, and private participants. It is difficult to apply in practice because of complex command structures, cultural and communications difficulties, and most of all because of the diverse interests involved.

The problem of clarity of intent is not aided by any military doctrine which treats multinational peacekeeping as an extension of purely national interests. A force commander will find it easier to achieve unity of effort with a clearly stated and broadly accepted intent which centres on de-escalation. Reducing the frequency and severity of violent incidents, then moving beyond that to increase trust and confidence between communities can be a unifying goal for military and civilian elements of a peacekeeping mission.

The goal of de-escalation can also be used to evaluate a second principle: minimum force, or use of force for self-defence only. If the impact of a narrow interpretation of self-defence is to increase the number of violent incidents (whether directed toward peacekeepers or opposing forces) then the rules of engagement should be reassessed.

The relationship between impartiality, consent, and the ability of the force to achieve de-escalation of violence is crucial, and was discussed at length in Chapter Three. The consent of the belligerents at the operational level gives peacekeepers the freedom to act at the tactical level against sources of violence from the "bottom up." Rogue elements, individuals and groups act on a variety of motives from hate and vengeance to calculated efforts to derail local progress for personal gain. Although consent can facilitate the third party's police role, it is more effective when the opposing forces can be induced to police their own transgressors. This not only reduces the burden on the peacekeepers, but is evidence of good intent which can be presented to the other side. When a belligerent party's consent is active and extends to controlling and policing its own transgressions, the conditions for broad offensive action have been established.

Deployment and Negotiation

Military doctrine presents two sorts of activities for peacekeepers: combat techniques, consisting largely of traditional military activities; and contact techniques which are more specific to peacekeeping operations. "Deployment and negotiation" are to peacekeeping as "fire and movement" are to war; they constitute the basic elements of the dialectic of defence and offense.

Defensive actions rest on the combat effectiveness of the peacekeepers whose primary function is to stop belligerents from shooting or moving against each other. The degree and pervasiveness of consent is the main determinant of the extent to which offensive techniques can be deployed. Consent to speak to a third party is an obvious prerequisite for negotiation. Beyond that, consent at the tactical level can lead to increased contacts between opposing communities. Consent at the operational level can facilitate more extensive local contacts, confidence-building measures, and inter-communal collaboration. Operational consent also permits the peacekeeping force to police violations at the tactical level, by deploying and using forces.

Just as movement is part of an effective tactical defence in war, negotiation is inherent in force deployments in peacekeeping. It occurs at every level, and is the first recourse of a section, platoon, or company thwarted in its duties. A second parallel with "fire and movement" is that negotiation is often most effective when carried out by a "unit" not in contact. The convoy commander who is stopped at a checkpoint can only negotiate with the checkpoint commander; his superior, or an uncommitted liaison officer, can try to reach the commander who gave the order to stop the convoy. In other cases, such as an ambush, the forces deployed may not be in a position to negotiate at all.

The most important lesson about deployment and negotiation is one which has not yet been committed to the pages of doctrine. In conventional fighting, forces move to enhance the effect of their fire, and fire to facilitate movement. In peacekeeping operations, forces deploy to support negotiations and negotiate to enhance and facilitate their deployment. Just as fire and movement must be tied to a larger concept of operations, so deployment and negotiation must support the overall plan of de-escalation. Contact skills are the vital ingredient which permit the advance of trust, confidence and inter-communal communications.

The conclusion of Chapter Three is that individuals require contact skills to handle incidents, staffs must use contact skills to manage force deployments, and commanders need contact skills to handle meetings effectively. All this contact, however, hinges on the effectiveness of the collective combat skills with which units handle incidents.

Limits to Military Action

Military peacekeepers are not confined to defensive action alone, but their ability to attack the roots of conflict is limited. Even defensive operations to stop belligerents shooting and moving are effective only following a cease-fire agreement, most commonly arrived at by civilian negotiators at the strategic or operational level.

It is in de-escalating beyond the stalemate of mutually hostile communities that the limits of military action are most apparent. The common military culture which permits soldiers to communicate with one another easily does not help to reduce tensions between belligerents, because the hierarchy of military discipline preserves mistrust and hostility between opposing forces. On the other hand, this same hierarchy and discipline is an important mechanism to control and prevent outbreaks of violence from the bottom up; a peacekeeping force finds it far easier to deal with a disciplined and cohesive force than a fragmented one with no clear chain of command.

There are two avenues to approach de-escalation of military tensions once the "main defensive battle" has been won, and forces are no longer actively moving against each other. The first, or direct approach, is from the top down. When agreement is reached at the strategic level, the opposing forces cease to be the enemy, and military confidence building measures and exchanges can be instituted from the top down as they were between NATO and former Warsaw Pact nations at the end of the Cold War.

The second, or indirect approach, is from the bottom up. It would be counter-productive to undermine the military chain of command, on whose coherence the effectiveness of peacekeepers partly depends. Therefore the bottom-up approach to tension reduction targets military commanders and the civilian communities from which soldiers are drawn. Military peacekeepers attempt to influence their counterparts, but civilian third parties are vital if civilian communities are to be reached effectively. This indirect approach has to be used with caution lest a perception arise that the peacekeeping mission is sponsoring "fifth columns" to undermine legitimate authority.

The Practice of De-escalation

The case studies and survey data presented in Chapters Four and Five permit me to conclude by answering the four questions posed at the outset: What sort of violence do peacekeepers face? What do they do about it at various rank levels? How to battalions and companies handle violent incidents? And how are campaigns of de-escalation conducted at battalion level and higher?

Violent Situations

The quantity and type of violence experienced by peacekeepers obviously varies not only between missions, but within missions over time. The same survey administered to Canadian troops in 1993 would yield different results if administered to the Jordanian battalion at the same time, or the Canadian battalions which preceded or followed.

The significance of types of violence, however, rests in the characteristics of the incidents which permit (or preclude) certain types of response. The most common types of violence experienced include exposure to mines, small-arms fire, indirect fire, physical threat and stone-throwing. As many as eight in ten peacekeepers of all ranks might experience this sort of violence in a mission like UNPROFOR. These are circumstances where the scope for contacting one's assailant varies, but is generally limited.

Peacekeepers face physical violence, often directed against them. They can defend themselves against this with basic combat skills, but rely on negotiations and contact skills to reduce the number and severity of incidents over time.

Rank Differences

There are significant differences in the balance of combat and contact experiences at different rank levels. A slightly larger proportion of NCOs than officers apply force, although overall the percentage is small—less than one in ten. In contrast, use of contact skills is widely reported and varies directly with rank—from about 15 percent of enlisted soldiers to about half of all officers.

These findings have implications for training and preparing units for complex peacekeeping missions. First, the widespread experience of violence reinforces the contention that all ranks need a thorough grounding in basic combat skills. Second, contact skills are increasingly important with increasing rank.

The third observation is apparent only from an understanding of how incidents are handled, and how their handling contributes to de-escalation. The exposure of peacekeepers on patrol to the dangers of mines, small arms fire, artillery and mortar shells occurs as part of a system of presence and escalating negotiations. The differences in contact and combat experiences by rank reflect, to some extent, the different functions of soldiers and officers. To officers, the managers of violence, falls the task of integrating military activities to control and de-escalate incidents.

Unit Tasks

How do battalions and companies handle violent incidents? The answer above is that they deploy (defend themselves) and negotiate. This can reduce violence in several ways. Two basic mechanisms are the "live-and-let-live" system, and deterrence.

The presence of a third party between belligerents reinforces the "live-and-let-live" system which can emerge between opposing forces. This relies on expectations about the behaviour of the opposing forces, and can be enhanced when the chain of command supports it. It becomes self-policing when violations are prosecuted by the violating side.

The potential for a broad interpretation of self-defence can act as a deterrent to belligerents, and can impose stability on volatile situations. This relies on expectations about the behaviour not of opposing forces, but of the third party. Information about the rules of engagement can be used to condition expectations about the peacekeepers' use of force. This in turn can contribute both to deterrence and to the "live-and-let-live" system.

These two basic mechanisms underlie the most common military tasks of peacekeepers at unit level. Patrolling, observation, recording and reporting information all support the stable "live-and-let-live" system. A robust capacity and demonstrated will for self-defence supports deterrence, but can backfire against a weak peacekeeping force.

Campaign Planning

How are de-escalation campaigns conducted at battalion level and higher? It is useful to distinguish between campaigns against "bottom-up" violence (like bored soldiers getting out of hand in Cyprus) and violence directed from the "top-down" (like the Medak pocket operation).

In the case of bottom-up violence, the problem is one of handling incidents at the lowest possible level and preventing escalation. By stifling individual incidents and using these as excuses for communication with (and perhaps eventually between) opposing forces, the cycle of escalating violence and hatred from the bottom up can be forestalled. Even if escalation can be forestalled in local circumstances, controlling incidents is not sufficient to change attitudes, even over a period of many years.

The key elements in planning for the control of bottom-up violence are a physical presence, contact and meetings at each level, and effective policing within the chain of command on the part of each opposing force. Isolated incidents can be handled at lower levels; linked and coordinated incidents have to be addressed at higher levels.

Top-down violence requires more coordinated campaigns. The term "top" is used loosely: whether the situation is the result of an initiative by a battalion commander, a brigade commander, or the highest leadership makes little difference to the soldier receiving an order. What distinguishes "top down" violence is that it occurs as the result of legitimately exercised authority at some level. This is the level which must be identified and pressured to resolve the incident. What the level is seldom obvious, and commanders' judgment will determine how fast and how high the contacts are escalated in an effort to find the right level to address the incident.

The aim of the contact is to make the responsible party *accountable* for the actions of subordinates. The key tool for establishing accountability is verifiable information. Reliable eyewitness reports, shell reports, crater analysis, patrol reports with photographic or video evidence, and independent investigations all contribute to accountability. The more immediate the accountability for the incident, the more easily the incident can be contained. This is comparatively simple when the UN is at fault. It is harder when the belligerents are at fault. The ire which a simple photograph can raise has more to do with accountability than the potential intelligence value of a photograph. Belligerents will destroy evidence, snipe at investigators, and deny culpability in blatant lies, because information is part of their war. Only consistent, fair, and carefully orchestrated campaigns can overcome this denial of responsibility for violent acts.

Theory, doctrine and experience suggest the key elements in campaigns against top-down violence. First, effective physical separation of factions makes the task a great deal simpler. Second, a public information campaign targeting the civilian population and efforts at long-term attitude change can be useful "multipliers" of military efforts. Combining the assurances of effective patrolling and pervasive presence with routine meetings at every level can systematically reinforce the "live-and-let-live" system. Experience also indicates that confidence-building can work even at the lowest levels.

Campaigns to reduce violence should take account of the context of the conflict, the type of violent incident, the characteristics of the participants, and the intervention strategies available. A history of antagonism and festering resentment are warning signs of impending escalation. Commanders should look for fatigue, voluntary yielding, conciliatory gestures and changing goals as indicators of possible de-escalation. The nature of most violent situations limits direct negotiations, so campaigns should be prepared to rely mainly on defensive deployments and indirect negotiations. Whether or not the participants are operating as part of a coherent chain of command will determine the degree to which they can be held answerable for their actions by their own side. The more fragmented the chain of command and the poorer the communications between levels of command (for whatever reason) the more manpower-intensive and time-consuming liaison and negotiation is likely to be.

Tactics, Techniques, and Procedures

Tactics, techniques, and procedures affecting soldiers' lives should be based on more comprehensive surveys of experience than I have presented here. Nevertheless, several conclusions can be drawn. The most obvious is that "procedures"—standard and detailed courses of action for performing a particular task—are not really applicable to de-escalation.

There are few standard situations in violent cross-cultural conflicts. I do not know how far one can generalize about conflict across cultural lines, and therefore there may be some doubt about any observations drawn predominantly from Eastern Mediterranean conflicts as these are. Nevertheless, certain common tactics and techniques for handling violent incidents can be picked from doctrine, surveys and interviews.

Tactics for Handling Violent Incidents

Direct and indirect fire can seldom be completely stopped even in comparatively stable conflicts. Fire has been effectively handled by fixing locations, preventing movement from these locations, keeping heavy weapons under observation (if possible, continuously), and by observing and reporting on target areas. Protests and pressure along the chain of command can help to reduce the incidence of unauthorized firing when there is concurrence by the belligerents.

Moves and attacks often require a battalion response. The use of a quick reaction force as a deterrent has been recommended in doctrine and routinely employed in practice. The effectiveness of any force deployed to prevent a forward movement or attack depends on thorough planning and a viable defensive option. The more convincing the military option, the less likely that it will be tested. The military option must be bolstered with maximum use of liaison officers and UNMOs to ensure that the capability and resolve of the UN is transparent to the opposing forces. The deployment must be demonstrably even-handed, not directed at one faction alone. The amount of force which is necessary as a deterrent will depend on the stakes and the relationships which have been cultivated, as well as on the motivation and capabilities of the belligerents.

Threats, intimidation and seizures must also be met with robust and resolute self-defence. The greater the incipient violence in a situation, the broader should be the interpretation of self-defence within the rules of engagement. The permissive rules might be broadcast as a part of a deterrent strategy. Firepower demonstrations like the one at the Maslenic Bridge can help to demonstrate capability and resolve.

The "four-fifths-of-a-tit-for-a-tat" rule can be used as a general guideline for achieving de-escalation. This suggests that one should lead with cooperation, be alert to feedback from an antagonist, punish (or at least avoid rewarding) coercion, and offer conciliation as a reward for de-escalation.

These tactics can be combined with the broader tactics of deployment and negotiation, as well as the "micro-level" techniques specific to particular combat or contact situations, which are liable to vary for each peacekeeping mission.

Conclusion

The operational art of peacekeeping is the combination of combat capability with effective contact at all levels to control and de-escalate violent incidents. Operational offensives take advantage of the stability which successful peacekeeping can bring about. Offensive action draws on advanced contact skills such as consultation, three-party mediation, and elicitive techniques. Language, culture and the target audiences for these efforts all suggest that operational offensives are a long-term civilian enterprise, with military assets in support.

Although this study is a useful start, it falls short of what soldiers, commanders and staff need to know to execute their missions effectively. They need more information about combat techniques, contact skills, and the integration of these tactics at the operational level.

First, there is still a lack of research on the effective handling of individual incidents. What is the best way for a peacekeeper to deal with a sniper? How should a section behave when it is surrounded by a hostile crowd? What should an officer and his driver do when they are held at gunpoint? These types of incidents and circumstances are diverse enough that procedures for such events cannot be developed. Different techniques need to be evaluated and compared. This body of knowledge then needs to be accumulated within each mission, and shared between missions to determine whether there are common lessons which can be applied across the very different military, political and cultural circumstances which peacekeepers face.

Second, the large body of literature which addresses negotiation, mediation, conciliation, problem solving workshops and other contact skills needs to be applied rigorously to the problems of peacekeeping. I have referred to both basic and advanced contact skills in this study, but I have not addressed adequately the application of these skills. A thorough investigation of how military peacekeepers use contact skills might pay dividends in training and operational planning, and might improve the integration of military and civilian efforts in offensive action.

Third, the vignettes offered in Chapter Five fall far short of comprehensive campaign descriptions. Complete and accurate descriptions of this type of campaign are a prerequisite to improving the integration of tactics at the operational level, and the coordination of operations to support strategies of de-escalation and conflict resolution. Unfortunately, units and headquarters are not well-placed to develop such histories. War diaries and logs are, in my experience, spotty records of events at best. For many contingents, they are inaccessible or non-existent. Teams of academic specialists observing missions might help, but are unlikely to capture the context of the mission accurately. The answer probably lies in serious professional research by soldiers themselves, undertaken as part of their mission, exactly as soldiers themselves have provided answers to the thorny questions of how best to attack bunkers, cross minefields, or defeat the latest tank.

Ultimately, much of peacekeeping is a soldier's job because only a soldier can do it. But Dag Hammarskjöld was only half right. Winning the peace is a team effort. Soldiers, civilians and above all our allies, the belligerent communities, must work together to defeat the violence.

Endnotes

1   Apocryphal, attributed to Napoleon.

Abbreviations

BATNA	"best alternative to a negotiated agreement"
CALL	Center for Army Lessons Learned
CANBAT	Canadian Battalion
CBM	confidence building measure
CGSC	Command and General Staff College
CSCE	Conference on Security and Cooperation in Europe
ICFY	International Conference on the Former Yugoslavia
JNA	Jugoslav National Army
JTF	Joint Task Force
LFC	Land Force Command
LFWA	Land Force Western Area
MEF	Marine Expeditionary Force
MFO	Multinational Force and Observers
NATO	North Atlantic Treaty Organization
NCO	non-commissioned officer
NGO	non-governmental organization
OOTW	operations other than war
ONUC	United Nations Operation in the Congo
ONUMOZ	United Nations Operation in Mozambique
OP	observation post
OSCE	Organization for Security and Cooperation in Europe
PVO	private voluntary organization
SQFT	*Secteur du Québec, forces terrèstres*

SRSG	Special Representative of the Secretary General
TOW	tube-launched, optically-tracked, wire-guided anti-tank missile
TTP	tactics, techniques and procedures
TUA	TOW-under-armour
UN	United Nations
UNAMIR	United Nations Assistance Mission for Rwanda
UNDOF	United Nations Disengagement Observer Force
UNEF	United Nations Emergency Force
UNFICYP	United Nations Force in Cyprus
UNITAF	United Nations International Task Force
UNIFIL	United Nations Forces in Lebanon
UNMO	United Nations Military Observer
UNOSOM	United Nations Operation in Somalia
UNPA	United Nations Protected Area
UNPROFOR	United Nations Protection Force
UNTAC	United Nations Transitional Administration, Cambodia

Bibliography

Books

Ashworth, Tony. Trench Warfare, 1914-1918: The Live and Let Live System. New York: Holmes and Meier, 1980.

Axelrod, Robert. The Evolution of Cooperation. New York: Basic Books, 1984.

Azar, Edward E. "Protracted International Conflicts," International Conflict Resolution: Theory and Practice. Sussex: Wheatsheaf, 1986.

Azar, Edward E., and John W. Burton International Conflict Resolution: Theory and Practice. Sussex: Wheatsheaf, 1986.

Bair, Andrew S. "Managing the Crisis in the Former Yugoslavia," in Peace Support Operations and the U.S. Military. Edited by Dennis J. Quinn. Washington, DC: Institute for National Strategic Studies, 1994.

Bandura, A. Aggression: A Social Learning Analysis. Englewood Cliffs: NJ: Prentiss-Hall, 1973.

Bard, M. and J. Zacker. The Police and Interpersonal Conflict: Third-Party Intervention Approaches. Washington: Police Foundation, 1976.

Bercovitch, Jacob, and Jeffrey Z. Rubin, eds., International Mediation: A Multi-Level Approach to Conflict Management. London: MacMillan, 1991.

Bercovitch, Jacob. Social Conflict and Third Parties: Strategies of Conflict Resolution. Boulder, Co: Westview, 1984.

Bowett, D. W. United Nations Forces: A Legal Study. New York: Praeger, 1964.

Boyd, B., and Bell, R. Crisis Intervention and Conflict Management Training in the RCMP: A Prescriptive Package. Ottawa: Ministry of the Solicitor General of Canada, 1985.

Brogan, Patrick. The Fighting Never Stopped: A Comprehensive Guide to World Conflict since 1945. New York: Vintage Books, 1990.

Burton, J. W. Global Conflict: The Domestic Sources of International Crises. Brighton: Wheatsheaf, 1984.

Burton, John. Resolving Deep-Rooted Conflict: A Handbook. London: University Press of America, 1987.

Camp, Glen D. "UN Efforts At Mediation." Perspectives on Negotiation, Foreign Service Institute, US Department of State, ed. Diane B. Bendahmande and John W. McDonald, eds, 127-137. Washington, DC: US Government Printing Office, 1986.

Cannetti, Elias. Crowds and Power. Harmondsworth: Penguin, 1973.

Choucri, Nazli and Robert North. Nations in Conflict: National Growthand International Violence San Francisco: W. H. Freeman and Sons, 1975.

Davies, J. C. "The J-Curve of Rising and Declining Satisfactions as a Cause of Some Great Revolutions and a Contained Rebellion." In Violence in America: Historical and Comparative Perspectives, eds. H. D. Graham and T. R. Gurr. New York: Bantam Books, 1969.

When Men Revolt and Why: A Reader in Political Violence and Revolution. New York: Free Press, 1971.

Deutsch, Morton. The Resolution of Conflict: Constructive andDestructive Processes. New Haven, CT: Yale University Press, 1973.

Greenwell, G. H. An Infant in Arms. London: Allen Lane, 1972.

Gurr, Ted ed. Violence in America: Historical and Comparative Perspectives. New York: Bantam Books, 1969.

Dollard, J., L. W. Doob, N. E. Miller, O. H. Mowrer, and R. R. Sears. Frustration and Aggression. New Haven, Ct: Yale University Press, 1939.

Druckman, Daniel. "An Analytical Research Agenda for Conflict and Conflict Resolution." In Conflict Resolution Theory and Practice: Integration and Application, ed. by Dennis J. D. Sandole and Hugo van der Merwe. New York: Manchester University Press, 1993.

Durch, William J., editor. The Evolution of UN Peacekeeping: Case Studies and Comparative Analysis. London: St. Martin's Press, 1993.

Eide, Asbjorn. "United Nations Forces in Domestic Conflicts." In Peace-Keeping: Experience and Evaluation — the Oslo Papers, ed. Per Frydenberg Oslo: Norwegian Institute of International Affairs, 1964.

Festinger, Leon. A Theory of Cognitive Dissonance. Stanford, CA: Stanford University Press, 1962.

Fetherston, A. B. Toward a Theory of United Nations Peacekeeping. University of Bradford. Bradford Books: Peace Research Report Number 31, February 1993.

Fetherston, A. Betts. "The Problem Solving Workshop in Conflict Resolution." In Peacemaking in a Troubled World, ed. Tom Woodhouse. New York: Berg, 1991.

Fisher, Roger, William Ury and Bruce Patton. Getting to Yes: Negotiating Agreement Without Giving In. 2d. ed. Harmondsworth: Penguin, 1991.

Gallagher, CSM James J. Low Intensity Conflict: A Guide for Tactics, Techniques, and Procedures. Harrisburg, PA: Stackpole Books, 1992.

Glasl, Friedrich "The Process of Conflict Escalation and Roles of ThirdParties." In Conflict Management and Industrial Relations, eds. Gerald B. J. Bomers and Richard B. Preston, 119-146. Boston, MA: Kluwer-Nijhoff Publishing, 1982.

Goldmann, Dr. Kjell. Peacekeeping and Self-Defence. Monograph No. 7, International Information Centre on Peacekeeping Operations, World Veterans Federation, 1968.

Gurr, Ted Robert. Minorities at Risk: A Global View of Ethnopolitical Conflicts. Washington, DC: United States Institute of Peace Press, 1993.

Harbottle, Michael N. The Impartial Soldier. London: Oxford University Press, 1970.Harman, Joan. "Peacekeeping in Somalia," Research Report 1663, US Army Research Institute, July 1994.

Hinsley, F. H. Power and the Pursuit of Peace: Theory and Practice in the History of Relations between States. Cambridge: Cambridge University Press, 1965.

Howard, Michael. The Lessons of History. London: Yale University Press, 1991.

International Peace Academy, Peacekeeper's Handbook. New York: Pergamon, 1984.

Jervis, Robert. Perception and Misperception in International Politics. Princeton, NJ: Princeton University Press, 1976.

Kaplan, Robert D. Balkan Ghosts: A Journey Through History. New York: Vintage Books, 1993.

Koestler, Arthur. The Ghost in the Machine. New York: MacMillan, 1967.

Koren, Leonard, and Peter Goodman. The Haggler's Handbook: One Hour to Negotiating Power. New York: Norton, 1991.

Kriesberg, Louis, Terrill A. Northrup, and Stuart J. Thorson, eds. Intractable Conflicts and Their Transformation. Syracuse: Syracuse University Press, 1989.

Lonergen, Stephen C., and David B. Brooks. The Economic, Ecological and Geopolitical Dimensions of Water in Israel. Victoria: Center for Sustainable Regional Development, 1993.

MacKenzie, Major General Lewis. Peacekeeper: The Road to Sarajevo. Toronto: Douglas and McIntyre, 1993.

Maslow, A. H. Motivation and Personality. New York: Harper and Row, 1987.

Miller, Robert, ed. Aid as Peacemaker: Canadian Development Assistance and Third World Conflict. Ottawa: Carleton University Press, 1992.

Mitchell, C. R. The Structure of International Conflict. London: MacMillan, 1981.

Mitchell, Christopher R. "Problem-solving exercises and theories of conflict resolution." In Conflict Resolution Theory and Practice: Integration and Application, eds. Dennis J. D. Sandole and Hugo van der Merwe. New York: Manchester University Press, 1994.

Morgenthau, Hans J. Politics Among Nations: The Struggle for Power and Peace. 5th ed. rev. New York: Knopf, 1978.

Moskos, Charles C., Jr. Peace Soldiers: The Sociology of a U.N. Military Force. Chicago, IL: University of Chicago Press, 1976.

Pillar, Paul R. Negotiating Peace: War Termination as a Bargaining Process. Princeton, NJ: Princeton University Press, 1983.

Pinch, Franklin C. "Screening and Selection of Personnel for Peace Operations: A Canadian Perspective," in Peace Operations: Workshop Proceedings, ed. David R. Segal. Alexandria, VA: US Army Research Institute, 1994.

Rikhye, I. J., M. Harbottle, and B. Egge. The Thin Blue Line: International Peacekeeping and Its Future. New Haven, CT.: Yale University Press, 1974.

Sandole, Dennis J. D. "Paradigms, theories and metaphors in conflict and conflict Resolution: Coherence or confusion?" In Conflict Resolution Theory and Practice: Integration and Application, eds. Dennis J. D. Sandole and Hugo van der Merwe. New York: Manchester University Press, 1994.

Savage, Grant T., John D. Blair, and Ritch L. Sorenson. "Consider Both Relationships and Substance When Negotiating Strategically," in Negotiation: Readings, Exercises and Cases, eds. Roy J. Lewicki, Joseph A. Litterer, David M. Saunders and John W. Minton. 2d. ed. Boston: Irwin, 1993.

Scott, John Paul. Aggression. Chicago: University of Chicago Press, 1958.

Snyder, Glenn H., and Paul Diesing. Conflict Among Nations: Bargaining, Decision Making and System Structure in International Crises. Princeton, NJ: Princeton University Press, 1977.

Van Creveld, Martin. The Transformation of War. New York: Free Press, 1991.

Volkan, Vamik. The Need to Have Enemies and Allies: From Clinical Practice to International Relationships. Northvale, NJ: Jason Aronson, 1987.

Waltz, Kenneth N. Theory of International Politics. Reading, MA: Addison-Wesley, 1979.

White, N. D. The United Nations and the Maintenance of International Peace and Security. New York: Manchester University Press, 1990.

Periodicals and Articles

Armstrong, G. P. "What the CIS Can Teach About Peacekeeping." Canadian Defence Quarterly, (October 1992): 47.

Apostolides, Costas. "Peace-building in Cyprus." Cyprus Mail. Sunday, 5 September 1993.

Azar, Edward E. "The Theory of Protracted Social Conflict and the Challenge of Transforming Conflict Situations." Monograph Series in World Affairs 20:2 (1983): 81-99.

Bair, Andrew "What Happened in Yugoslavia? Lessons for Future Peacekeepers." European Security 3:2 (Summer 1994).

Bartos, Ottomar J. "How Predictable Are Negotiations?" Journal of Conflict Resolution 11:4 (1968): 481-496.

Bendor, Jonathan. "Uncertainty and the Evolution of Cooperation," Journal of Conflict Resolution (1993).

Bercovitch, Jacob. "International Mediation: A Study of the Incidence, Strategies and Conditions of Successful Outcomes." Cooperation and Conflict 21:3 (September, 1986).

Bercovitch, Jacob. "Third Parties in Conflict Management: The Structure and Conditions of Effective Mediation in International Relations." International Journal 60:4 (Autumn 1985): 737-752.

Bercovitch, J., Theodore Anagnoson and Donnette L. Wille. "Some Conceptual Issues and Empirical Trends in the Study of Successful Mediation in International Relations," Journal of Peace Research 28:1 (February, 1991): 7-18.

Claude, Inis L. "United Nations Use of Military Force," Journal of Conflict Resolution 7:2 (June 1963).

Claude, Inis L. "The United Nations and the Use of Force," International Conciliation. 532 (March 1961): 325-384.

Deutsch, Morton "Conflict Resolution: Theory and Practice." Political Psychology. 4:3 (September 1983): 431-453.

Diehl, P. F. "When Peacekeeping Does Not Lead to Peace: Some Notes on Conflict Resolution." Bulletin of Peace Proposals. 18:1 (1987) 7-53.

Diehl, P. F. "Peacekeeping Operations and the Quest for Peace," Political Science Quarterly 103:3 (Fall 1988): 485-507.

Dobbie, Charles. "A Concept for Post-Cold War Peacekeeping." Survival 36:3 (Autumn 1994).

Dworken, Jonathan T. "Rules of Engagement: Lessons from Restore Hope." Military Review (September 1994): 27-28.

Eiseman, Jeffrey W. "Reconciling 'Incompatible' Positions," The Journal of Applied Behavioural Science 14:2 (1978): 133-150.

Eiseman, Jeffrey W. "A Third-Party Consultation Model for Resolving Recurring Conflicts Collaboratively," The Journal of Applied Behavioural Science 13:1 (1977): 303-314.

Finger, Seymour M. "The Maintenance of Peace," Proceedings of the Academy of Political Science 32:4 (1977): 195-205.

Fisher, Roger. "Dealing with Conflict Among Individuals: Are There Common Principles?" Psycho-analytic Inquiry 6:2 (1986): 143-153.

Fisher, Ronald J. "Prenegotiation Problem-Solving Discussions: Enhancing the Potential for Successful Negotiation," International Journal 44 (Spring 1989): 442-474.

Fisher, Ronald J. "The Potential for Peacebuilding: Forging a Bridge from Peacekeeping to Peacemaking." Peace and Change 3:2 (1993).

Fisher, Ronald J. and Loraleigh Keashly. "Third Party Interventions in Intergroup Conflict: Consultation is not Mediation," Negotiation Journal 4:4 (October 1988): 381-393.

Fisher, R.J. "The Potential Complementarity of Mediation and Consultation within a Contingency Model of Third Party Intervention," Journal of Peace Research 28:1 (February 1991).

Galtung, J. "A Structural Theory of Aggression," Journal of Peace Research 1 (1964).

Galtung, Johan. "Three Approaches to Peace: Peacekeeping, Peacemaking and Peacebuilding." Impact of Science on Society. (1976).

Johan Galtung and Helge Hveem. "Participants in Peacekeeping Forces," Cooperation and Conflict, (1976).

Gagnon, Mona Harrington. "Peace Forces and the Veto: The Relevance of Consent." International Organization. 21:4 (Autumn 1967): 812-836.

Harbottle, Michael. "Strategy of Third Party Intervention," International Journal 35:1 (Winter): 118-131.

Herbert, Major Paul H. Deciding What has to be Done: General William E. DePuy and the 1976 Edition of FM 100-5, Operations. Leavenworth Papers, Number 16, Fort Leavenworth: Combat Studies Institute, (1988).

Hill, B. J. "An Analysis of Conflict Resolution Techniques: From Problem-Solving Workshops to Theory," Journal of Conflict Resolution 26:1 (1982): 126-153.

Homer-Dixon, Thomas F. "On the Threshold: Environmental Changes as Causes of Acute Conflict," International Security (Fall 1991): 76-116.

Kaplan, Robert D. "The Coming Anarchy," The Atlantic Monthly. 273:2 (February 1994): 44-76.

Kende, Istvan. "Twenty Five Years of Local Wars," Journal of Peace Research (1990): 5-22.

Lanir, Zvi. "The 'Principles of War' and Military Thinking," Journal of Strategic Studies, 16:1 (March 1993).

Last, D. M. "Peacekeeping Doctrine and Conflict Resolution Techniques," Armed Forces and Society 22:2 (Winter 1995/1996): 187-210.

Last, Major D. M. "Cooperation between Units and Observers," Peacekeeping and International Relations 23:5 (September-October 1994): 4.

Loizos, Peter. "Intercommunal Killing in Cyprus," Man 23 (1988): 639-653.

Mandell, Brian S., and Ronald J. Fisher. "Teaching Ideas: Training Third-Party Consultants in International Conflict Resolution." Negotiation Journal (July 1992): 259-271.

Prein, Hugo. "A Contingency Approach to Conflict Intervention." Group and Organization Studies 9:1 (March 1984): 81-102.

Reuter and Associated Press. "Bosnian Serbs Hijack Medical Supplies: Dangerous Showdown Develops as Troops Refuse to Leave Demilitarized Zone" Toronto Globe and Mail (Tuesday, 18 October 1994): A2.

Rupesinghe, Kumar. "Building Peace after Military Withdrawal," Bulletin of Peace Proposals 20:3 (1989): 243-251.

Smith, Richard. "The Requirement for the United Nations to Develop an Internationally Recognized Doctrine for the Use of Force in Intra-state Conflict," Strategic and Combat Studies Institute, The Occasional. Number 10 (1994).

Stein, Janice Gross. "Getting to the Table: The Triggers, Stages, Functions, and Consequences of Prenegotiation," International Journal 44 (Spring 1989): 475-489.

Suhrke, Astri. "Pressure Points: Environmental Degradation, Migration and Conflict." Occasional Paper of the Project on Environmental Change and Acute Conflict, Number 3 (March 1993).

Volkan, V. "The Need to Have Enemies and Allies: A Developmental Approach." Political Psychology 6 (1985): 219-245.

Wall, James A. "Mediation: An Analysis, Review and Proposed Research," Journal of Conflict Resolution 25:1 (March 1981): 157-181.

Government Documents

Boutros-Ghali, Boutros. Agenda for Peace. New York: United Nations, 1992.

Canadian Forces Publication B-GL-301-303/FP-001 Operations Land and Tactical Air, Volume 3: Peacekeeping Operations. First Draft. Ottawa: Supply and Services, November 1994.

Center for Army Lessons Learned, CALL. Newsletter 93-8: Operations Other Than War, Volume IV: Peace Operations. US Army Combined Arms Command, Fort Leavenworth, Kansas, December 1993 .

Center for Army Lessons Learned. Somalia, Special Edition No. 93-1, US Army Combined Arms Command, Fort Leavenworth, Kansas, January 1993.

Conference on Security and Cooperation in Europe, "Charter of Paris for a New Europe" 1990.Conference on Security and Cooperation in Europe, "Peaceful Settlement of Disputes Annex 3".

Conference on Security and Cooperation in Europe. "Report of the CSCE Meeting of Experts on Peaceful Settlement of Disputes," Valetta 1991.

Conference on Security and Cooperation in Europe. "Prague Document on the Further Development of CSCE Institutions and Structures," CSCE Second Meeting of the Council, Prague 1992.

"Convoy Operations," Dispatches: The Army's Lessons Learned Newsletter, 1:1. Kingston, Ont: Canadian Armed Forces, Land Force Command, November 1994 .

Fawzy, Ehab Rapporteur. "Comprehensive Review of the Whole Question of Peace-Keeping Operations in all their Aspects" Report of the Special Committee on Peace-Keeping Operations. Draft, A/47/92-23222 3101c E, 1 June 1992.

Hederstedt, Colonel Johan, Lt Col Jrn Hee, Maj Nils W. 0rum, Maj Simo Saari, Capt Olli Viljaranta. Nordic UN Tactical Manual, Volumes 1 and 2. Gummerus Kirjapaino Oy, Jyväskylä, 1992.

Joint Warfighting Center. Joint Task Force Commander's Handbook for Peace Operations. Pre-printing copy Fort Monroe, VA: Joint Warfighting Center, 1995.

Joint Publication 1-02. Department of Defense Dictionary of Military and Associated Terms, Incorporating the NATO Glossary of Terms and Definitions. Washington: Department of Defense, 1 December 1989.

Memento sur l'espace yougoslave, République Français, Ministère de la défence Février 1994.

Russian Peacekeeping Center. UN Peacekeeping Operations: Organization, Conduct and Logistics, Functional Duties of Personnel. Moscow, 1994.

United Kingdom Army Field Manual. Wider Peacekeeping Fifth Draft Revised, 1994.

United Kingdom Army Field Manual. Volume V, All Arms Tactics, Special Operations and Techniques, Part 1: Peacekeeping Operations. London: Her Majesty's Stationary Office, 1988.

United Kingdom Army Field Manual. Keeping the Peace. Volume 1 London: War Office, 1963.

United Nations. Blue Helmets: A Review of United Nations Peace-Keeping. New York: United Nations Department of Public Information, 1990.

United Nations. United Nations Peacekeeping: Information Notes — Update May 1994. UN NY: Peace and Security Programmes Section, 1994.

United Nations. Training Guidelines for National or Regional Training Operations, 1991.

United Nations Department of Peacekeeping Operations Training Unit. Junior Ranks Handbook. New York: DPKO, 1994.

United Nations Department of Public Information. United Nations Peacekeeping Update: May 1994. New York: Department of Public Information, 1994.

United Nations Secretary General. Report of the Secretary-General on his Mission of Good Offices in Cyprus. United Nations MSF 9577-08, S/24472, 21 August 1992 with attachment, Set of Ideas on an Overall Framework Agreement on Cyprus MSF 9577-08, 1992.

United States Army Field Manual FM 100-5. Operations. Headquarters, Department of the Army, June 1993.

United States Army Field Manual FM100-23. Peace Operations. Washington: Headquarters, Department of the Army, December 1994.

United States Foreign Military Studies Office. Russian-United States Guide for tactics, techniques, and procedures of Peacekeeping Forces During the Conduct of Exercises. Fort Leavenworth, KS: Foreign Military Studies Office, 1994.

Unpublished Materials

Bloomfield, Lincoln P., and Allen Moulton. CASCON III: Computer Aided System for Analysis of Local Conflicts. User Manual Beta Test Version 2.0 preliminary version, Cambridge, MA: MIT Center for International Studies unpublished with addendum 7 dated 7 January 1991.

Canadian Armed Forces After Action Report extracts CANBAT 1 Report on Medak Pocket Operations 15-21 September 1993.Canadian Broadcasting Corporation. "Sniper," CBC Sunday Morning, aired 27 February 1994.

Department of National Defence. Peacekeeping Interview Programme, Survey data.

Douglas, BGen Ian. "Peacekeeping Operations," Department of National Defence, 1850-1/90 SPA/DCDS 16 Jan 1991.

Eyre, K. C. ADGA Systems International, "Anecdotal Data from CANBAT 2 12ᵉ RBC General Peacekeeping Survey," Eyre, K. C. ADGA Systems International "Anecdotal Data from UNPROFOR OP HARMONY CANBAT 1 1 R22ᵉR General Peacekeeping Survey," Peacekeeping Interview Program. Ottawa, October 1993 - April 1994.

Force Mobile Command Headquarters Staff. "Negotiation in Peacekeeping," Unpublished staff paper prepared circa 1973.

Grinberg, Jaque. "The UNPROFOR Mandate," Civil Affairs HQ UNPROFOR, unpublished paper, 14 February 1994.

Kretchik, Major Walter E. Peacemaking and Operational Art: The Israeli Experience in Operation "Peace for Galilee." Fort Leavenworth: School of Advanced Military Studies Monograph, 1992 .

Malabotta, Melita Richter. "The Balkan Irrationalities," Paper presented at the Freidrich Naumann Foundation and the Janus Pannonius University International Conference on Reasons and Consequences of the Crisis in the Former Yugoslavia, 1-4 December1994, Pécs, Hungary.

Nordick, G. W. LCol. 1994 "Low Level Negotiations: Operation Harmony Croatia. Presentation of Techniques," 16pp.

Oehring, Colonel G. J. "Between Brothers: Some Views from a Year in Croatia," unpublished paper.

Robertson, Major Victor M. The Relationship Between War and Peacekeeping. Fort Leavenworth: School of Advanced Military Studies Monograph, 1992.

Troop Information Pamphlet for the Balkan Peninsula, 1992. Unpublished paper issued to US troops.United Nations Department of Peacekeeping Operations. Command and Control Review. 9 November 1993.

Other Sources

Interviews:

Baxter, LCol James, United Kingdom

Boynton, Maj Frank, United States Marine Corps

Calvin, LCol Jim, Canadian Armed Forces

Chubbs, Capt Lloyd, Canadian Armed Forces

Couture, Col Alain, Canadian Armed Forces

Crowell, Capt Kevin, Canadian Armed Forces

Dallaire, MGen R.A., Canadian Armed Forces

Davidson, LCol John, Canadian Armed Forces

Duncan, Col Alistair, United Kingdom

Eaton, Maj Doug, Canadian Armed Forces

Eyre, Dr. Dana, United States Army (Reserve)

Johanssen, LCol, Sweden

Itani, Maj Ted, Canadian Armed Forces (Retired)

Lafortune, Capt J.G., Canadian Armed Forces

Lasan, Ms. Dolores B., Chief of Mission, UNHCR in Cyprus

Landry, LCol, Canadian Armed Forces

Lemay, Maj J.P., Canadian Armed Forces

MacKenzie, MGen Lewis, Canadian Armed Forces (Retired)

Mahmoud, Maj Ali Shdayfat, Jordanian Armed Forces

Makulowich, Maj Marv, Canadian Armed Forces

Milner, MGen Clive, Canadian Armed Forces (Retired)

Moore, LCol David, Canadian Armed Forces

Nordick, LCol Glen, Canadian Armed Forces

Oehring, Col G.J., Canadian Armed Forces

Olmstead, Maj Lance, Canadian Armed Forces

Rittiman, Maj Olivier, Ingénieurs du Légion Étrangère, France

Smith, Maj Brad, Canadian Armed Forces

Sray, LCol, United States Army

Taylor, Maj Barry, Canadian Armed Forces

Windsor, Maj Phillip, Royal Air Force

Vadeboncoeur, Capt, Canadian Armed Forces

Viljarantam, Capt Olli, Armed Forces of Finland